JOURNEYS IN FAITH

A 1-Year Weekly Devotional

Presented by R. S. Dugan

For information contact :
SPIRIT & TRUTH
PO BOX 1737
MARTINSVILLE, IN 46151
spiritandtruthonline.org

Book and Cover design by Rebekah Milestone
ISBN: 978-1-0880-4244-1

First Edition: December 2022

10 9 8 7 6 5 4 3 2 1

INTRODUCTION

by R. S. Dugan

Throughout the several decades I've spent alive on this earth, one of the lessons God has taught me (and retaught me...and retaught me AGAIN) is how faithful He is.

I have often kept prayer journals and other documentation on hand so that I could go back and see for myself just how much the faithfulness of God has been present in my life. Though He often shows Himself in such incredible, earth-shattering ways, sometimes I forget to stop and be in awe of Him. Or I become so used to His presence in my life, I become almost blinded to it. Neither of these are things I ever want to get comfortable with.

So I make notes. And I remember. And when I forget, then the things God had me write are there to remind me.

I had a similar experience as I moved toward my second year of motherhood; when I was in a season of overwhelm at just how much my toddler needed me, God brought me back to a seemingly innocuous exchange between two characters in a novel He had inspired me to write five years prior.

Half a decade later, He was still teaching me His truths from a throwaway line inspired by His wisdom.

What you hold in your hands with this second one-year devotional is a reflection of the same endless faithfulness of our Heavenly Father. In many ways, this book is a trail of footprints through the lulls and upheavals of life. It is an honest and utter reflection of the journey God took me on during good times and bad—the lessons He needed to teach me. And the ones that He encouraged me to teach to others when the time was right.

I am in a different season of life now, all these years later, but I am no less excited to share these things with you. And I am wholly confident that even the most seemingly-innocuous, forgettable lines may be precisely what you need to hear.

God knows. And He can show you, just as He showed me.

By the way—you don't have to read our devotionals in any particular order. The beauty of God's wisdom is that He can teach us lessons right where we are with exactly what we've got, with no need to be aware of the order of things. While no one quite walked the same journey that I did when writing a series of blogs that would one day become a devotional, I trust that He will work in your heart—just as He worked in mine as I wrote them—to bring forth the message that needs to be seen and received.

And may God be with you as you see. And as you receive.

God bless you!
R. S. Dugan

NEW YEAR, NEW ME!

HAPPY NEW YEAR!

At the beginning of every year, the world unites around one word: "resolutions." With the start of another circle around the sun comes the sense that anything is possible, and many people feel empowered, even invincible enough to tackle goals that even one day previous seemed overwhelming.

Most resolutions revolve around the betterment of one's life, usually through health goals or the laying aside of bad habits that affect their ability to live their best life. This transformation is often championed with the phrase "New year, new me!"

But for the devoted Christian, the mindset of "new year, new me" is a day-by-day endeavor. While studies show that as much as 54% of people give up on the "new me" by June of each year, this isn't the way Christians are instructed to live.

As followers of Jesus, we are told to "put off the old self that belongs to [our] former way of life and that is being corrupted because of deceitful desires [...] and put on the new self, which has been created in the likeness of God in true righteousness and holiness." (Eph. 4:22, 24)

What a powerful, life-changing command! Our solutions to the problems that come with a sinful nature in a fallen world are not found in a 30-day workout regimen, a decluttered house, or even a healthier diet. Our transformation comes from putting off what was old and dead and putting on what is new, and living in the likeness of God. This includes trading lies for truth, anger for peace, thieving for generosity, gossip for words of encouragement, and more.

As we move ahead, we must ask ourselves this: are my resolutions too narrow? Am I dreaming too small? Am I fixing cosmetic issues in my life—whether large or small—and ignoring the deeper spiritual realities?

This is not to say that physical wellness, a healthy environment, and other goals cannot better us as people and as followers of Jesus. But it's wise to ensure we are in a continuous state of spiritual renewal, from darkness to light, just as we work to renew and transform our outer environment.

When we center our resolutions, both annually and daily, around embracing the instructions of Christ—that we would live a life transformed, taking off the nature of the old man and putting on the new—that is when we will experience a truly blessed and transformative year, with a truly *NEW ME!*

This Week's Prayer: God, thank You for another year full of opportunity to spread Your truth and become a better disciple! Help me to make the most of every day for You! Amen.

JESUS CHRIST & THE PLAN OF REDEMPTION

I OFTEN THINK ABOUT HOW beautiful and deep and rich the story of God's redemption plan and His purpose for the ages truly is. It can even seem incomprehensible by mortal standards:

How many threads had to be woven in.

How crucial the steps were.

How much was at stake and what had to happen to bring about the salvation of mankind.

Book of Ephesians lays out the history of mankind's fallen state, the change from darkness to light for those who believe, and the commission for the redeemed going forward. There was purpose in this great plan for unity and the creation of one entity, the Body of Christ—erasing the division between Jew and Gentile—to which even Jesus himself wasn't privy until after his resurrection!

And yet, even not comprehending the entirety of God's purposes, Jesus trusted his Father enough to lay down his life to see that plan fulfilled.

I often find myself reading and thinking a lot about Jesus, trying to really comprehend what he went through mentally, physically, and spiritually in the days leading up to his death. Having comprehended more deeply than even his closest friends the agony and torture he would endure, he had to have *so much faith* in the power of God's plan in order to go through with it. To drink from that cup he didn't want, his trust in his Father's wise purposes had to be unshakeable. And to move in step with God, who even then kept the broader scope of the Gentiles' part in the plan of redemption safeguarded in Himself, Jesus had to trust that in everything he knew and everything he didn't know, God was faithful.

The need for redemption, the call for a savior, the sacrifice he made—all of this rose to a crescendo in the life of Jesus Christ. In his perfect model of trust and love.

How important is God's purpose for the ages? How magnificent are His plans? How important is the peace and redemption brought about by His will?

Our Lord thought it was worth *dying* for.

So I hope you'll also join me in celebrating the great purposes of God of which he, and we, are all part. This great symphony of the ages, which unites us as one; with Jesus Christ as our head, who modeled the way of sacrificial love and trust, in fulfilling *his* part in God's purpose for the ages.

This Week's Prayer: Yahweh, thank You for Your amazing plans and purposes! Thank You for giving me a part in those plans. Help me to fulfill everything to which You've called me, in a way that glorifies You. Amen.

WHY ADOPTION MATTERS

ADOPTION. IT'S A LONG AND intricate journey for any family who chooses to take that road, with a spate of background checks, fees, and rules involved. And that's all besides the emotional rollercoaster that comes with bringing someone else's child permanently into your family. Unlike fostering, which is often a temporary situation, adoption means that child becomes your own, for better or for worse, forever.

The more I've studied and read personal accounts and immersed myself in the intricacies of adoption, the more the allegories in Ephesians and Romans about this process have stood out to me.

In Roman culture, adopted children were considered *chosen*. Because the adopting family knew what they were getting into—the adoptee's traits, blemishes, and often their strengths and weaknesses—lawfully, there was no going back once the adoption was fulfilled. The adopted child was a part of the family and that was that, no takebacks. This differed greatly from Jewish culture where adoption was basically unheard of, as blood children were the only ones carrying on the family name. For that reason, the New Testament books written to Jewish converts use sonship phraseology while the books to Gentile converts focus on the adoption aspect of our belonging to God.

In in our modern culture, adoption takes a child with an uncertain future and places them permanently in the arms of those who will care for them. They become grafted on to that family as if it was their own. That's the exact image God wanted to evoke when he called us *adopted* in Ephesians 1:5 and Romans 8:15. Because of this adoption into sonship, we now call God "Father", and we share in the inheritance of His family.

What an awe-inspiring privilege! This is why understanding the concept of adoption as it was in the Gentile days of old truly matters.

God knew *exactly* what He was getting into with each of us—He knew our traits, our blemishes, our strengths and weaknesses—and still He gladly adopted us into His family. He welcomed us with open arms even knowing the unique adjustments that would take place as we struggled (and still do!) with taking our place in His family and all the personal change and growth that entails.

This notion moves me to tears: that God would give us such love, such status, such a family that we are no longer aimless and homeless but carry His name. We are adopted, chosen children of the Most High! Praise God!

This Week's Prayer: Yahweh, thank You for adopting me into your family! Help me to never lose sight of how special it is that You CHOSE me and we will never be separated! Amen.

PAID BY THE BLOOD

I HAVE RARELY FELT SO horrible in my life as when I've hurt, offended, or angered someone unintentionally. I have a bad habit of acting in a moment without thinking through the consequences of my choice. Sometimes, by the grace of God, this works out well for all involved. But there are times when I find out after the fact that this caused a major dilemma, distress, or inconvenience for someone else because I crossed a boundary I had no place going over. In a sense, I have now "transgressed" against them.

Webster's Dictionary defines "transgression" as "an act that goes against a law, rule, or code of conduct; an offense." Another term for this is a "trespass."

More than anyone else, I know I've done this to God. We all have.

Way back in the day, when sacrifices were required of the Israelites, there were different sacrifices as penance for intentional versus unintentional sin. One was given in penance for a willful act; the other covered a multitude of trespasses against God which one might've done and not been aware of. The beautiful thing is that the blood of Christ covered *all* our transgressions, our trespasses, the places where we've unknowingly crossed the boundary and entered into sin.

When the eyes of our understanding are opened and we become aware of all the sin we are capable of, life starts to feel like a minefield. Everywhere we step, there's another explosion of bad behavior waiting to go off! At times it's difficult to know how badly we've fallen short in ways we don't even know about. My dad taught me a great prayer for this: "God, forgive us for any way we have sinned against You, Your Son, or Your people today."

Even when we are on our absolute best behavior, offenses will happen, both against our fellow humans and against our Creator. But what a blessing it is to know that there was not one sacrifice for our intentional sin and another for those offenses we weren't aware of. *The blood of Christ paid it all.* And why? According to the riches of God's grace, by His own wisdom.

What else can we be but thankful for all that He and Jesus Christ have done for us—that they even forgive us for the sins we don't know to repent of! We are so very, very loved.

This Week's Prayer: Jesus, Thank You for your sacrifice! Help me to never lose sight of the importance of that endless love. And God, forgive me for any way I have sinned against You, Your Son, or Your people today. Help me to do better tomorrow. Amen.

WHO & WHAT DEFINES YOU?

IN SEPTEMBER 2018, MY HUSBAND and I made a commitment to pursue reading the Book of Ephesians together, over and over, until we gained the best possible understanding of its many wonderful lessons. Having read it twice in the

Holman's and once in the Revised English Version, we decided to pick up The Message version.

I've always had a love/hate relationship with The Message, but there's no denying it brings a different depth of perspective to passages we might otherwise grow blind to with the small variances between standard translations. While flipping through The Message for a preliminary overview of Ephesians, I came across a line I had to pause and reread many times, and each time it resounded louder and deeper in my soul.

In a loose translation of Ephesians 1:11, The Message reads: "It's in Christ that we find out who we are and what we are living for."

It might be for personal reasons that this translation stuck with me. I'm no stranger to trying to figure out who I am and what I'm living for. At that time in 2018, it seemed most of my peers were on a similar journey of self-discovery. And yet this translation of Ephesians 1:11 brought me so much peace as I read and reread it.

It's in *Christ* that I find out who I am and what I am living for. Whoever he says I am, that's me. No need to go on a journey...I've already been found, seen, defined.

And what am I living for?

Simple. For God and Christ. Whatever they tell me to do, that's my purpose, and what they tell me to live for, that is my total commission. No more questioning, wandering, or confusion.

It's amazing how so simple a phrase can help clear the fog of confusion that comes with navigating this fallen world. Those without Jesus as a guide often flounder through attempt after attempt to discover their identity and purpose, throwing themselves into fleeting causes in hopes of finding *something* to live for—something that may also tell them who they are. Even as a Christ-follower, I've struggled with trying to find out what defines me.

And there it was, right on the page: *in Christ*, we find who we are and what we're meant to live for.

Time to get busy living.

This Week's Prayer: Yahweh, thank You for the gift of Your Son who helps me know who I am and what I should be living for! Help me to live in a way that's pleasing to You! Amen.

SERVING THE ONE ABOVE ALL

IN THE FIRST CHAPTER OF Ephesians, there is so much emphasis placed on two particular subjects: Jesus's current status and identity, and our identity and status through our union with him. Having been sealed, redeemed, and bestowed with a guaranteed inheritance and every spiritual blessing through

Christ, it can be almost too easy to get caught up in what *we've* gained as laid out in Ephesians 1 and entirely miss Christ's part in this:

Ephesians 1:20b-23

[God] raised [Christ] out from among the dead and seated him at his right hand in the heavenly *places*, [21]far above every ruler, and authority, and power, and those having dominion, and every name that is named, not only in this age but also in the one to come; [22]and he put all things in subjection under his feet and appointed him *as* the head over all things for the church, [23]which is his body, the fullness of the one who fills all things in every way.

It wasn't until I finally took the time to read this Scripture slowly that it hit me: Christ has been placed above *every* ruler, and authority, and power, and everyone and everything in dominion who ever existed or ever will exist. And he is also the head of us, the Body. I know we know that as Christians, but do we really *know it*?

How many times do we put other rulers, other figures of authority, ahead of Christ—intentionally or not? How often do we make someone else's opinion paramount over Jesus's words spoken to us, his commands to his Body?

We serve a Master who is not just a little above, but *far above* every ruler in this age. There is nothing that ought to surpass our determination to follow his commands and his example, to serve how and when and where and in the way he tells us to. Fulfilling our functions as members of the Body of Christ is the end to which we have been blessed and empowered. This is not just for our enjoyment but also for the betterment of the whole world, to the end of exhorting fellow believers and bringing more souls into the family of God.

Nothing could be more important than the great commission from our Lord, who is over all things in this church of which we are members and disciples.

This Week's Prayer: Yahweh, thank You for placing such a great head of Your Body! Please help me to serve You and Jesus well and to never place any other ruler, power, or authority before him in my life. Amen.

SEEING GOD'S GLORY:
THROUGH HUSBANDS & WIVES

I'VE RARELY SEEN A PASSAGE of Scripture as plucked over and examined for current application as the section in Ephesians 5 that speaks to husbands and wives. In many instances, a "battle of the sexes" ensues as men and women struggle to define the topic of submission in this context. Interestingly, in many cases both sides opt for the more self-serving interpretation of this pertinent passage, when in fact the subject of submission throughout Ephesians 5 and into Chapter 6 is purely sacrificial, the entrusting of one's own wants and needs to another—as is the husband's role of laying down his life for his wife.

Ultimately, the examples in Ephesians 5:21-32 are a submission/sacrifice interplay that mirrors the way of Christ with the Church.

Submission

While verse 21 reminds us that in some way or another, *everyone* is subject to someone else (wives to husbands, husbands to Christ, children to parents, servants to masters), particular emphasis is placed on the wife's submission to the husband. Not woman's submission to man, but specifically the healthy spousal relationship.

Why this emphasis? And why did God specify that this submission must play out between a wife and her own husband in particular? Because that submission parallels a beautiful spiritual reality: the subjection of the Church to Christ, following his leading in everything.

Married women play an important role in the story of salvation that I would daresay no one else can: through our behavior, we model the way for others and for the Body of Christ at large to see how we *all* ought to submit to Christ. Our charge from God is that we would walk out our relationship with our husbands in such a godly manner that our intimacy and submission reflect the intimate way the Church interacts with Christ via our wholehearted, trusting submission and his provision for us.

Sacrifice

Equally as important as the model of submission is that of sacrifice. Married men are God-called to live a life that is completely not about themselves. Instead, each man is charged to care for his wife's needs above his own to the extent of dying for her—and willingly, as Christ did. It was out of sheer, unselfish love for people and dedication to the will of the Father that Jesus died on the cross. With an equally unselfish and God-fearing love, husbands are called to place the wellbeing of their wives above all others'.

When married men live in this role, they model Christ for other believers and particularly for their own families. They show the fealty of the Son to the Father and the compassion that marked Jesus's whole life from start to finish. Their charge from God is to love their wives even as themselves.

When we truly grasp how hard the body fights to keep itself alive even in the worst conditions—the ways God engineered us to persevere beyond what may seem survivable—this ordination on the role of husbands becomes even more imperative. The husband is to fight for, nourish, cherish, rescue, and redeem his wife as he would his own life—even at the risk of dying in her place. This is no easy thing to do when survival instinct is built into humankind, often urging us to put our own needs above any else's. For the husband, that isn't an option in God's eyes.

So, why did God mark out these roles so clearly? Because when both sexes fulfill these God-ordained roles, the submission/sacrifice interplay is complete. Trust is made whole because the wife is safe in submission knowing her every need will be cared for, and the husband is safe in sacrifice knowing that he has the respect of his help-mate, the created answer to life's first problem (Gen. 2:18), who will not demand unjust sacrifice of him but will work in tandem to recreate the model of Christ and the Church.

One of my friends summed this entire aspect up profoundly when teaching from this section of

Scripture. She said that "submission flows from intimacy." In the case of husbands and wives, when intimacy and trust is fostered, submission from the wife to the husband—and from both parties to one another as members in particular of the Body of Christ—flows naturally.

That is the ultimate outworking of healthy submission and sacrificial love, of devotion and respect: these married Christian couples present a profound and unique example of spiritual realities that can hardly be found anywhere else.

Why is it so important to God that we are faithful to model these relationships in a godly fashion? Why did He take the time to lay out the rules of submission and responsibility for each side of these three particular relational aspects in Ephesians? I believe one very crucial reason is this: when we fail in these areas, we misrepresent a portion of that beautiful mystery mentioned in 5:32.

Think back to Numbers 20, when God became angry with Moses because instead of speaking to a rock to bring water from it, Moses struck it with his staff, something God had him do on a previous occasion. I always struggled with that passage as a young Christian—why was God's punishment against Moses so harsh for what seemed like so small an infraction?

It wasn't until much later that I realized the mistake Moses made that so grieved God: the symbol of speaking to the rock after having struck it the previous time was a foreshadowing of Christ, who after being struck for our transgressions (the first rock) would then offer living water to all who asked (spoke to him, the second rock.)

In much the same way, when we fall short of loving and respecting our spouses, when we provoke our children or disrespect our parents, when we're unkind to those in service to us or rebellious and insolent to those we serve, we are misrepresenting the godly structure that parallels and exemplifies spiritual realities. Like Moses striking the rock, we distort the will of God and become poor examples of the perfect story *He* is trying to tell through us.

So whether single or married, son or daughter or parent, leader or follower, we should *all* pay special attention to the sections of Scripture that tell us how to be in godly relationship with one another. It's imperative for us as followers and witnesses of Christ that we do our very best to be good examples and accurate models for the deeper, godly truth that our Heavenly Father intended for our relationships to be.

This Week's Prayer: Yahweh, thank You for the great spiritual truths You reveal through the sacred bond of marriage. Help me to become increasingly more aware of the beauty of Your creation, and fulfill my role in it! Amen.

SEEING GOD'S GLORY:
THROUGH PARENTS & CHILDREN

IT WAS A YOUNG MOTHER around my age who opened my eyes to a whole new angle of the parent/child relationship as laid out in Ephesians.

She and I were discussing the journey of motherhood, and I asked her if there were any spiritual realities that she became more aware of after becoming a mother. Her answer stuck with me: "Obedience. I understand better why it honors God when we obey Him out of trust because I feel honored when my children trust and obey *me*."

Think deeply on these verses:

"Children, obey your parents in the Lord, for this is right. Honor your father and mother (which is the first commandment with a promise), so that it goes well with you, and you live long on the earth."

In addressing the husband/wife aspect of Ephesians, we saw how each of these temporal relationship packages in Ephesians 5:21-6:9 models a greater spiritual reality. With that in mind, what are some of the lessons we can glean from this one?

The parent/child relationship on earth is a mirror of the parent/child relationship we have with our Heavenly Father.

While, in this segment, God adds that parents must be obeyed "in the Lord" (i.e. when their moral compass is sound), we know that with Him, all things are godly. Therefore, just as it's plainly stated that it's right to obey our earthly parents in what is righteous, we're meant to obey God in all things because *He* is righteous. Period. *This is right.*

In a similar parallel, when we honor Him—just as when we honor our mortal parents—life goes much better for us.

Another aspect to this section is that *through* showing honor to our parents—and thus to the natural order and structure of the family as God designed it, which is host to a plethora of spiritual examples and types—we honor God. This section is rife with both paralleled and direct paths to blessings!

Similar to the way the submission/sacrifice interplay between husbands and wives is a holy charge to model the spiritual reality of the Church and Christ, the parent/child relationship shows the honor/discipline interplay between God and us, His children.

The way parents treat their children has a formative effect on the child's view of God.

As a young girl, I heard it said many times that a woman's relationship with her earthly father will profoundly impact her outlook on God.

We often subconsciously project a perception onto eternal God that has its roots in how we perceive our earthly dads. I believe this segment of scripture speaks to that for both male *and* female children.

God gives a warning for parents not to provoke their children to wrath—i.e. antagonize or exasperate them simply to get a reaction. They're to train their children in a godly way, in the discipline and instruction of the Lord.

From this, we can see the way that *God* behaves with us as *His* children: the things He tells us to do, the paths to avoid, and the rules to abide by are not to antagonize or anger us, or to provoke us to wrath! His purpose by His instruction is always to train us up and bring us to a place of better understanding Him so that our obedience flows from trust and wholehearted submission, not from grudging anger or because of injurious provocation.

Thus, the way that parents teach, discipline, and interact with their children is meant to model a godly love: with concern for the spiritual and physical wellbeing of the child rather than with any interest in goading or upsetting them.

As *The Message* version of Ephesians 1:18-19, exhorts in Paul's prayer:

Ephesians 1:18-19
I ask—ask the God of our Master, Jesus Christ, the God of glory—to make you intelligent and discerning in knowing him personally, your eyes focused and clear, so that you can see exactly what

it is he is calling you to do, grasp the immensity of this glorious way of life he has for his followers, oh, the utter extravagance of his work in us who trust him—endless energy, boundless strength!

In the previous segment on husbands and wives, we reflected on this quote: "submission flows from intimacy." This principle applies perfectly to the parent/child relationship, as well: when we comprehend God's love for us and why He gives us the commands and commissions He does, why He interacts with and teaches us in so many ways, we come to fellowship with Him on a deeply personal, relational level of intimate love and trust, and our submission to Him flows naturally from that.

The parent/child relationship, built on obedience, trust, training, and love, is one of the most profound and beautiful examples of God's relationship with His people.

It's up to each of us to wholeheartedly pursue a healthy, godly relationship within these parameters—both with our earthly parents and with our Heavenly Father.

This Week's Prayer: Yahweh, thank You for the beautiful realities of Your love for us modeled through the family system. Please help me to honor You through how I interact with my family! Amen.

SEEING GOD'S GLORY:
THROUGH MASTERS & SERVANTS

OF THE TRIAD OF RELATIONSHIPS covered in Ephesians 5-6, the master/servant interplay can be the hardest to bring into terms applicable to the current culture. Possibly the closest we have is employer/employee, although that relationship doesn't have quite the same overtones. Perhaps the best way to distill the concept down into a broader application is between "one in command and one who follows those commands."

Why is it so important that those in charge and those who obey them invest in a healthy relationship? To properly answer that question, we have to go all the way back to Ephesians 1.

The Master Model

The first chapter of Ephesians tells us that when Jesus was raised from the dead, God placed him "far above every ruler, and authority, and power, and those having dominion, and every name that is named, not only in this age but also in the one to come; and he put all things in subjection under his feet and appointed him as the head over all things for the church." (Eph. 1:21-22)

What this means for us is that Jesus is our Master. We are subject to him in all things. He is the model of the perfect Master, Lord, and One in command: he is sinless, impartial, wise, just, and loving.

To that end, masters (those in command) are meant to exude those same qualities as imitators of the One who is Master over all. There's no space for threats and domineering because this behavior distorts the perfect master/servant relationship we have with our brother Jesus. When someone in a position of power over others uses that position to make threats, abuse authority, or come down harshly on those subject to them, they are misrepresenting the one who is both the servant's master and theirs.

The Servant Model

Ephesians 6 actually tells us point-blank that in servitude, we are to display qualities of "[obedience] to those who are [our] lords according to the flesh, with fear and trembling, and in sincerity of heart" as if to Christ (Eph. 6:5). The Greek word translated "sincerity" here has the meaning of "Simple goodness, which gives itself without reserve, 'without strings attached', 'without hidden agendas.'"

In other words, wherever we are working, whoever is in charge over us, we're to serve in a way that is honoring to our God and to Christ. Thus, we lead by example, showing our genuine reverence, trust, and pure-hearted obedience not just toward our earthly "bosses" but to the One who is their boss as well as ours.

In all things, we have the opportunity to model our obedience to our Master Jesus through our conduct toward those in authority. Ephesians 6 tells us to conduct ourselves this way, "knowing that whatever good anyone does, he will receive the same back from the Lord."

Similarly, Colossians 3:23 tells us "Whatever you do, work from the depths of your soul, as for the Lord and not for people."

What these few verses ultimately show is that whether we are in positions of service or leadership, we have a responsibility to conduct ourselves in a way that honors God and Christ. We're to show restraint, respect, humility, sincerity and fairness, and love.

To do any less shows a fault in the posture of our hearts as servants of Christ, or else it misrepresents the nature of the Master himself—the one who is seated above all and is through all and in all.

This Week's Prayer: Yahweh, thank You for the profound aspects of our relationship with Your Son that are revealed in places like Ephesians 6. Please help me to always work and serve wholeheartedly in a way that glorifies and honors Jesus, who is Lord over all! Amen.

TEARING DOWN THE DIVIDING WALL

EPHESIANS 2 PAINTS A BEAUTIFUL illustration of one of the most profound realities that came about with Jesus' sacrifice: with the fulfillment of the Law, and through his death, Christ put to death the hostility between the Jews and Gentiles by becoming the bridge that spanned the gap between them.

Through Christ, rather than through the Law, both Jew and Gentile could attain salvation as part of one unified Body of Christ.

In the two thousand years since Jesus died, one thing has become very evident: humankind has not lost their pre-Jesus penchant for putting up dividing walls, and Christianity is not immune from this either. 44,000+ denominations, anyone?

While it can be easy to love and accept and applaud the tearing down of the hostile wall between Jews and Gentiles—a cultural friction most of us have never experienced for ourselves—what about the denominational walls we perpetuate within the Body of Christ?

There's a verse in Matthew 19 discussing the matter of divorce, where Jesus says, "What God has joined, let no man separate." (Matt. 19:6) Sometimes, within our own denominational biases, Christians mentally "force divorce" on Christ and *his* Bride, the Church, by considering one group or denomination more or less holy and even more or less likely to truly b saved.

We raise the barrier of hostility and try to redefine the boundaries of what the Body of Christ *is*, based on who thinks like us, talks like us, acts like us, believes like us.

But we are all reconciled to Christ by the cross. There is only one Body of Christ, and we don't get to say who is part of it any more than the Jews got to decide whether the Gentiles were coheirs, or vice versa.

This is God's family, and we are all privileged to be a part of it. Let's not sully the family name by erecting walls and causing division, resurrecting hostility and destroying peace.

Jesus died to make two groups into one. Even if our doctrine is different, we are still *One Body*. So to the best of our ability, let's make sure we're living in reconciliation and peace, because *none of us* are foreigners or strangers anymore; we are all members of the household of God.

This Week's Prayer: Yahweh, thank You for being a God of unity, not division! Please help me to tear down any walls I put up in my own life that separate me from Your people. Help me to model the unity of Your household in my walk with You. Amen.

WALKING ALIVE

IT SEEMS LIKE NOWADAYS, ZOMBIES are everywhere. From movies and television to clothing, accessories, books, and costumes, the "undead" genre has gained something of a cult following.

What are zombies, by the way? Basically, they're human husks whose only desire is to feed on flesh (and apparently create jump-scares for viewers). They shamble aimlessly around a stricken landscape looking for their next meal, moaning and shrieking except when they're in stealth mode for maximum scare effect, popping up in the most inconvenient moments and devouring their victims. Other than to consume, they have no real direction in life—or afterlife. They just exist.

Funny to think that spiritually, we all start out like "zombies."

Ephesians 2 tells us that as alive as we are physically, spiritually we all started out as dead people walking around in our transgressions and sins—the wages of which are indeed death (Rom. 6:23)—subject to the ways of this world and the corrupt one who rules it. We were all the spiritual undead shuffling through life, looking for something to consume according to our fleshly desires with a kind of rabid anger. Our only desire in that state was to feast on what made us feel good, what the Apostle Paul calls "the passions of our flesh."

Yet at some point, every child of God chose to reach out for the cure for this death. We decided that rather than being the walking dead, we wanted to be the walking *alive*. We wanted a better place than our stricken landscape, and a better hope than to be enslaved to the ways of a dystopic, post-Fall world.

We wanted a purpose in life under the calling of the only one who could truly turn our dead state to life.

So we cast off our shackles of mindless consumption and embraced the gracious gift of God for spiritual life, awakening, and salvation. We are no longer purposeless consumers, but active members of a living force to take back the world and bring light to it.

For some of us, this redemption happened so early in life we don't really remember what it felt like to live in that place of spiritual death. For others, that time is still near and vivid, sometimes soberingly so. But what unites us all is that, as God tells us, we *all* come from this same place of death into life—whether we remember it clearly or not. We *all* were once dead in transgressions and sins; now we are *all* made alive in Christ, who by laying down his own sinless life on the Cross forged a bridge across that gap from death to life for us.

Now, in Christ, all who believe—regardless of their origins—have been rescued from the state of death and brought into a life of purpose, with a glorious future seated in the heavenlies with the one who saved us.

On the toughest days of living your Christian faith, when there is division or devastation or when you simply feel like you're walking dead again, remember your true spiritual identity: you are alive in Christ, as are all your brothers and sisters in the One Body.

You no longer wander aimlessly, devoid of holy spirit, bereft of purpose and future. You have been given a new life through your belief in the resurrected Christ. And it's time to start walking alive!

This Week's Prayer: Yahweh, thank You for sending Your Son to redeem us from death to life. Help me to walk in the fullness of that life and to bring others into it as well! Amen.

BE STILL

AH, THE NEVER-ENDING, WILD race of life. I can smell it from the moment I roll out of bed every day. It has the tinge of fresh coffee, open windows, the breath of a hungry cat or three (pleasant), and the smiles of my son. From the time I get up in the morning until it's back to bed, I rarely stop moving. And sometimes not even then.

Twice as hectic as the pace of life is the pace of mind. If I'm not actively working, I'm *thinking* about it...the million things I did today, want to do still, will do tomorrow. And I know I'm not alone in this crazy pace of living. There seems to be no end to the demands on our time, our minds, our peace.

Why is it so hard to pause? To breathe? Well, because if we don't do it—whatever "it" may be— who's gonna? If we aren't handling things, they'll fall apart. Who's going to win the battles of life if we aren't in them—constantly, endlessly at work?

And yet.

Though we were designed to work—to tend the Garden, to rule over the creatures, to labor for a living—we were created in the image of a Holy God who also took a day of rest.

Do *we* rest? Or do we stop moving physically, but race ahead a mile a minute mentally? Is our rest truly *rest*, or is it a forced physical pause until we can get moving again?

When I think of this concept, I flash back to a scene in *Star Wars Episode I: The Phantom Menace*. In a three-way duel between Jedi mentor and apprentice Qui-Gon and Obi-Wan and their nemesis, the Sith Lord Darth Maul, there comes a point mid-battle where the three are separated from one another by laser barriers. It's a forced pause. There is no moving forward—not yet.

Darth Maul scowls and paces. Obi-Wan stands tense, ready for anything. Yet Qui-Gon kneels and closes his eyes. For him, it's not just a forced physical pause, but a mental settling to recenter himself for the battle yet to come.

How often when at rest do we truly go still? Do we truly strive for peace? Or do we instead pace and tense up and even rattle the bars of this cage, fighting the pause enforced on us.

Why don't we lean into it? Embrace it?

Stillness is more than rest. It is that mental settling. It's inner quiet where we actually *stop* all the work, all the frenzied racing, all the harried rushing. Where the heart and mind are at peace and we let go of the things that need to happen tomorrow, today, *right this very second or else.* Let the battle go for a moment, and breathe.

It's in those moments of stillness that we connect on a deeper level with our Creator. Where it becomes easier to hear His voice. When it stops being about us and everything *we need to do* and becomes clearer than ever what He wants for us and from us.

"Peace, be still," Jesus said to the tempestuous waves.

"Be still, and know that I am God," Yahweh tells us through the Psalms.

It can sometimes feel like failure or laziness to lean into a pause, into rest, into peace. But it's not. It's refreshment for the body and restoration for the soul. It helps us keep a healthy perspective on the fact that we are not the masters of the universe, the ones responsible to keep the cogs spinning. It brings us face to face with the One whose plans and purposes we are walking out—and when we embrace Him, embrace the rest and peace He has in store for us, we are better able to understand that we are not facing this hectic, wild, fast-paced life and all its challenges and have-tos and deadlines and needs alone.

"I will fight for you," our Heavenly Father says. *"You need only be still."*

This Week's Prayer: Yahweh, thank You for fighting for me and for all those who call on Your name! Please help me to take pauses, to reset my mind, and to truly be still with You. Amen.

A PRAYER FOR YOU

HAVE YOU EVER FELT LIKE there was a particular subject God was pressing you to take notice of? Something that just came up over and over in a myriad of ways?

At one point in my life, I felt like God was encouraging me to pray more; to make prayer my default when I was anxious or helpless or angry. To make a conversation with Him my go-to in all situations.

So I did! And the more I dwelled on (and in!) prayer, the more I saw how it is often a universal "Christian connector." We may disagree on matters of doctrine and practice, but prayer is one of those things any Christian can do for any other Christian at any time and it feels *intimate*. It makes you feel heard and seen by your fellow Christian and by the Creator of the Heavens and the Earth. In those moments of prayer, the feeling of God's presence where two or more are gathered in Christ's name feels like the truest reality that's ever been.

There are a lot of prayers in the Bible. Some are expressly named as such (The Lord's Prayer, Mary's Prayer) and some are not. There are two that became particularly special to me: Jesus's prayer on the night he was betrayed in John 17, and Paul's prayer for the Body of Christ in Ephesians 3.

John 17

This entire prayer from Jesus over his disciples is just so powerful. If you haven't read it ever, or even in a while, I encourage you to go read it now. Read it in multiple versions. Read it daily. This is Jesus's heart for those who were with him then, those of us who are in him now, and those who have yet to accept him.

Look at these words: "I am not asking for these alone, **but also for those who will believe in me through their word, so that they can all be one, just as you, Father, are in union with me and I in union with you, that they also can be in union with us, so that the world may believe that you sent me.**" (John 17:21 REV)

Over 2,000 years ago, Jesus prayed this prayer *for you*. How incredible is the love in this passage? You have been prayed over by saints you have never met, and by Jesus himself, in times before you existed.

Ephesians 3

Knees deep in Ephesians 3 during a fellowship weekend in 2018 was the first time I truly, clearly, and without a shadow of doubt heard the voice of God and conversed with Him. It was the most powerful few hours of my existence and it all stemmed from Ephesians 3, and particularly Paul's prayer at the end. I read it in multiple versions – particularly the REV Bible and *The Message* – and somewhere between the two, I understood how POWERFUL these words are. Not only the power of this prayer Paul prayed over the believers in Ephesus, but how it transcends the centuries as a prayer for *us*.

Between the different perspectives brought to light by *The Message* and *The REV*, I comprehended not only God's and Christ's love for us as witnessed by this prayer, but its life-changing effects and why it's so important for us to grasp it. Like Paul, I couldn't help but fall on my knees before the Father, awestruck and humbled to tears by the sheer vastness of what has been done for us, through Christ.

Prayer is so important...the prayers we say, and the prayers that are prayed over us, both by our fellow believers now and by the ones who walked this world before us. That feeling you experience when a brother or sister in Christ takes a moment to pray for you is a sensation that pours down through the ages.

In closing, I want to share the passages of Ephesians 3 that brought me to my knees. Maybe they'll resonate for you the same way—maybe they won't. But I hope you take the time to read and truly soak in these life-giving words of truth.

And know that in all earnestness, in all honesty, in all Christian love, this is my prayer for each one of you who reads this. My brothers and sisters in Christ. My holy family:

(**The MSG**) My response is to get down on my knees before the Father, this magnificent Father who parcels out all heaven and earth. I ask him to strengthen you by his spirit—not a brute strength but a glorious inner strength—that Christ will live in you as you open the door and invite him in. And I ask him that with both feet planted firmly on love, you'll be able to take in with all followers of Jesus the extravagant dimensions of Christ's love. Reach out and experience the breadth! Test its length! Plumb the depths! Rise to the heights! Live full lives, full in the fullness of God.

God can do anything, you know—far more than you could ever imagine or guess or request in your wildest dreams! He does it not by pushing us around but by working within us, his spirit deeply and gently within us.

(The REV) For this reason I bow my knees to the Father, from whom every family in heaven and on earth is named, that according to the riches of his glory he would grant you to be strengthened with power by his spirit in the inner man so that Christ would dwell in your hearts through trust; *and that you,* having been rooted and grounded in love, are fully able to comprehend with all the holy ones what is the breadth and length and height and depth, and thus to know the love of Christ that surpasses knowledge, so that you are filled with all the fullness of God.

PRAY IT LIKE YOU MEAN IT

NOW THAT WE HAVE AGREED on the importance of prayer, let's talk about the importance of not letting your promise to pray just be a promise, or your words just be words.

I'm as guilty of this as anyone: after hearing about something someone is going through or hoping for or is in need of guidance about, I tell them I'll pray for them. I always mean it. I truly do.

And then I...don't actually do it. I get distracted. And I forget.

Most of us who do this do it with the best intentions to actually pray. But at the same time, "I'll be praying for you" has in some ways also become a phrase without meaning—a pat answer when we're at a loss for anything else to say.

But our words are important, as is the promise of prayer. Prayer is powerful, it's vital, and we should not waste the opportunity to do it. Nor should we promise that we will and then neglect that promise.

I write these words to myself as much as to anyone else: whatever it takes, we need to hold to our word when we promise people we'll pray for them. We need to stop and pray in the moment we make the promise, and then we need a way to remember to do it again, and again, fervently and often. Try:

- Reminders on your phone
- A post-it note on the bathroom mirror
- An entire prayer board hung in the office
- Joining a prayer email group or prayer fellowship where you pray about things together
- A hand-written list

- Praying with a spouse, family member, or friend

Whatever you need to do to remember to pray for the things you promise, I deeply encourage you— as I encourage *me*—to do it. Don't let a promise to pray simply become a fill-in-the-blank for when you're at a loss for any other words, but be forever mindful of what an important promise you're making. And stick to it.

This Week's Prayer: God, please help me to be intentional in my prayers! Please bring to remembrance all the things I've committed to pray for so I can continuously devote them to You. Amen.

15

ROOTED & GROUNDED IN LOVE

DESPITE A LIFELONG FASCINATION WITH the beauty of the flora God has provided for us to tend and enjoy, I have never considered myself a gardener. I have a bit of a black thumb; most of the flowerpots I receive will be dead inside a month, no matter how meticulously I water them. I suppose there's a good reason God put Adam and Eve in the Garden, not me.

But then one day, much to my initial chagrin, our office team adopted a little orchid we dubbed "Jaffa." At the time, I was picking out orchid-sized coffins in my head, giving the thing until spring before it withered away to nothing.

Yet for three years, and despite a few missed weekly feedings, Jaffa thrived, doubling in size and blooming multiple times, each one providing months of wondrous beauty after which she returned to hibernation. Given my initial lack of orchid knowledge, I was tempted to toss her out after the first blossoms fell, but with persistence and routine feedings even when she seemed by all accounts dead, Jaffa continued to reawaken.

During her budding and hibernating phases, Jaffa sprouted a copious number of "air roots"—little green tendrils that often far exceeded the height of her orchid pot. And as wild as Jaffa's air roots grew, her roots in her soil, which we faithfully watered, were also deep.

When we'd had Jaffa for about two years, we decided to experiment with our communal botany skills by keeping TWO orchids alive. Enter Cheva, a little orchid my mom won at a bridal shower, who came along already dazzling with unique blossoms.

But unlike Jaffa, Cheva's potting was not good; not only that, but his roots both in and out of the soil were thin, shriveled, and sickly looking. Despite our best efforts, once those first gorgeous blossoms fell from Cheva's stalks, he never bloomed again.

People talk a lot about the importance of where you're going in life—in essence, how you're blooming—but not as much attention is often given to your roots. Jaffa was only able to flourish because her roots were strong and nourished, and that in turn nourished the rest of her. She grew because she was grounded. She was empowered from the soil up.

In this way, we're not so different from orchids.

Ephesians 3:17-18 tells us that we must be *rooted and grounded* in love in order to comprehend the dimensions of Christ's love for us; and through that love, we become empowered to grow and love others in a more productive way. The love we must be rooted in refers to both God's love for us, and our love for Him, for Christ, and for our fellow believers. When we are rooted in this love, anchored in it, fed by it, we are able to flourish and mature.

What nourishes the soil *you're* planted in? Are you rooted and grounded in love? Does love, both received and given, feed and empower you to expand beyond where you started, to grow twice as high as the boundaries that contain you, to accept and also offer greater and greater love?

That's the reality God yearns for us to live in: one of comprehending Christ's love, experiencing it, and spreading that same love to others. When we are rooted in these dimensions of love, we will be filled with the fullness of God. And what a wonderful state that is! But this doesn't just happen overnight. It takes time and care to cultivate our roots. A lot of it depends on our soil and how we're planted. We must remember that we grow when we're well-grounded. It's the only way to thrive.

This Week's Prayer: Yahweh, thank You for providing the good soil of love for Your people to root in! Please make me aware of what I can do to become even better rooted and grounded in love, so that I can truly experience the dimensions of Christ's love and be filled with the fullness of You! Amen.

BLESSED WITH EVERY SPIRITUAL BLESSING

ONE OF MY MOM'S FAVORITE rituals is what she calls "Happy Tuesday" presents. Giving in general is one of the many, many ways she expresses love, and she decided that gift-giving shouldn't be constrained to holidays or birthdays. So if she sees something she thinks will bless you, chances are you'll receive it on a random Tuesday.

I've always thought her giving spirit is a crystal-clear reflection of God's heart toward His children. There are plenty of people, both believers and non-believers, who assume God is among the capricious pantheon of cross-religious deities who take without giving and exist only to be worshipped and feared.

But that's not our Heavenly Father. He loves us as the perfect Dad: with discipline, delight, and even the giving of gifts.

Ephesians 1:3 sums up this giving side of God's nature as it addresses what became of us when we confessed Jesus as Lord: "[...] The God and Father of our Lord Jesus Christ, who has blessed us in *union with* Christ with every spiritual blessing in the heavenly *places...*"

WOW! Because of our union with Christ, God has lavished on us EVERY spiritual blessing in the heavenly places! A portion of that refers to a future time—like the fullness of our salvation, for which we now have the gift of holy spirit as a "down payment" until it's made complete—but there are current spiritual realities that were also sealed within us at the moment we became God's own.

The REV Bible commentary lists a few of these blessings:

"We have already seen that we were crucified with Christ, died with Christ, were buried with Christ, and were raised with Christ. Some of the other blessings that Ephesians lists as our having by virtue of being "in Christ" are: blessed in Christ (Eph 1:3); chosen in him (Eph 1:4); being the praise of the glory of God's grace (Eph 1:6); redeemed (Eph 1:7); claimed as God's possession (Eph 1:11); sealed with the promised holy spirit (Eph 1:13); raised up and seated in the heavenlies (Eph 2:6); created (Eph 2:10); made near (Eph 2:13); created into a new man (Eph 2:15); being built into a sanctuary of God (Eph 2:21, 22); Gentiles are fellow heirs, fellow members, and fellow partakers of the promise (Eph 3:6); and, forgiven (Eph 4:32). All of these blessings and more are by virtue of us being "in union with" Christ; part of his Body."

All of this became our individual spiritual reality when we came into union with Christ! And God continues to bless us in ways seen and unseen, to the praise of His glory.

What better way to prove that we are cherished, important, and beloved of God than that He has given us so many gifts at the moment we believed, lavishing us with these gracious things from redemption and forgiveness to holy spirit power and the titles of HIS CHILD, and SAVED.

Happy Tuesday to us!

This Week's Prayer: Yahweh, thank You for all the spiritual blessings You've bestowed on me, Your beloved child! Please help me always make the most of those blessings for the good of all. Amen.

WHY THE TRUTH MUST BE SPOKEN IN LOVE

DURING MY TEEN YEARS, I had a slew of friendships in which I was the target of verbal abuse.

No matter what names I was called or what snide remarks came my way, I just took it, thanks to a deplorable lack of self-worth. I remember my mom calling out one of these instances when a girl bluntly chided me for being "fat," to which my friend shot back, "What? I'm just telling the truth!"

I've continued to encounter that mentality into my adult years, though it's less often directed at me. "I'm just telling it how it is," "You gotta face facts," or "Just call a spade a spade" are a few I hear on an almost daily basis; and coming from a faith in which truth is paramount, that can be a difficult approach to argue against.

Speaking the truth has almost become a salvo to say whatever we want—that is, whatever we *know* or *believe* is true. And in many circles, even Christian ones, you'll find it doesn't matter if the way it's said is hurtful, disheartening, or even alienating. The truth offends, after all, so that's on you—right?

Yet the Bible itself calls to question the motive of our hearts when we speak. Do we tell truths just to be heard, or do we tell them to the end that others receive them, consider them, and if need be, change in healthy ways because of them? Are we using these truths as a word fitly spoken, or as a weapon? Are we clanging cymbals speaking in the tongues of men and angels without love?

Scripture braids the concept of truth *spoken in love* with maturity in Christ. I had never really put those two concepts together before, and yet there it is, right on the page:

Ephesians 4:15-16
"But speaking the truth in love, we are **to grow up in every way** into him who is the head, Christ, ¹⁶from whom the whole body, being fitted together and held together by every supporting ligament, with each individual part doing *its* proper function, produces the growth of the body with the goal of building itself up in love."

How about that? Growing up into Christ and fulfilling our function in his Body doesn't happen unless we're coming from a place of love. And doesn't that just make sense? After all, the head of the Body is Christ, and the Head of Christ is God; and if God is love, then to imitate Him, all that we do must come from love. Even the way in which we express truth.

So consider:

- If you have an admonishment for someone, if it's to be rightly spoken, it must come from a place of love, not from the root of self-righteousness or self-service.

- If you're confronting someone, it must be done with love, for the loving reason, not merely to pick a fight or justify yourself in an angry outburst or personal opinion.
- If you're speaking to a reformed brother about past sin, watch how you speak to him and ask yourself, "Am I addressing him with love, or from a place of unresolved hurt?"
- If you're calling out someone's flaws or shortcomings, is it because you want to see them grow and change, or is it for a personal motive?

In any of these cases, you may be speaking truth—but the *reason* and the *way* you speak that truth truly matters to God. It is by the love of Christ that we model the truth of Christ and the way to Christ. No human form of truth or love will do.

Learning to act from godly love rather than human motivations is an ongoing growth. This must be checked and balanced against 1 Corinthians 13, which hallmarks the wonderful qualities of a true and holy love.

And why is it so important that we act from a place of love—that we remain deeply rooted and grounded in it, as Ephesians 3 says? Because only love can bear, believe, hope, and endure through all things.

So if we are to bring the image of our Heavenly Father to everyone we meet, and endure the trials of life, relationship, confrontation, frustration, and this fallen world, we must ensure that we are rooted and grounded in love, speaking the truth in love, from the abundance of a heart full of godly love, so that we edify all those to whom we bring the Gospel as living epistles.

This Week's Prayer: God, please help me to be mindful of my motivations as I speak to those around me. Help me to act from a position of love as well as truth in all I say and do! Amen.

NO LONGER STRANGERS

DEEP WITHIN THE HUMAN HEART, there is an intrinsic desire to be seen, known, and loved. We crave intimacy—*"into-me-see"*—and seek it out it in many places. And just as few things are as rewarding as emotional and heartfelt intimacy with those we hold dear, few things are as damaging as to be unseen, unknown, and unloved. The sense of detachment that creeps out of such feelings has many times led the hopeless to take their own lives.

I have felt this personally on many occasions. Over the years, God has brought it plainly to my attention that my greatest weakness and the biggest bruise on my heart is when I'm made to feel like I'm expendable. And I know many others who feel the same way.

Humankind was made for relationship, and when we feel excluded from it, we often become depressed, despondent, and desperate. We recognize within ourselves the need to belong to something bigger, for our hearts to be cradled in hands broader than our own.

When that need goes unmet, it creates a void that nothing else can fill.

Have you ever attended some kind of social function where you didn't know anyone? Or perhaps where you knew some people, but they were too busy with other acquaintances to pay you any mind? Likely there was some discomfort involved, some awkwardness, even the feeling that you didn't belong there and couldn't wait to leave. There is a deep disquiet that comes from feeling like an outsider or a stranger. It can even drive us to question if there is something "wrong" with us that places us on the "outside" of everyone else—all these people around us who seem to have things figured out.

Whether you have ever experienced this estranged feeling in a social climate or not, the truth is that the status of "outsider" was once reality for *everyone*. We were strangers to God, outsiders of the Chosen People, until Christ came along. In his death, Jesus tore down the dividing wall that kept us on the outside looking in, and he has shepherded his followers into the Father's fold. Our belief in Jesus brings us into a *new* reality—one of acceptance and understanding, of intimacy and family.

Ephesians 2:19 tells us we are "no longer strangers and foreigners, but you are fellow-citizens with the holy ones and members of the household of God." In *The Message* version, this is translated: "You're no longer wandering exiles. This kingdom of faith is now your home country. You're no longer strangers or outsiders. You *belong* here, with as much right to the name Christian as anyone."

What a profound reality. Our days of wandering in the wilderness are over. We have found our home country. We *belong*.

This is true of us all, a reality which we must embrace with our whole hearts, let it fill and fuel us to understand our worth and purpose. The Creator of the Universe sees, knows, and loves each of us.

Jesus Christ opened the path for an intimate relationship with him and with God from which we will never be separated.

In the household of God, there are no strangers. We belong. We are family. We are *home*.

This Week's Prayer: Yahweh, thank You for abolishing the "outsider" title from my life! Thank You for instating this family where we all belong. Please help me to live wholly in that truth, now and always! Amen.

TO WALK WORTHY

WHEN I WAS IN SIXTH GRADE —the only year I went to public school—I earned an award in my Language Arts class. It was called the Edger Allen Poe Award for Excellence, and it was given to the most promising young writer in the grade.

In the eyes of most, it probably wasn't a very prestigious award, but I remember how proud I was to hold it in my hands and how validated I felt that someone besides my parents had seen potential in my stories.

From that day forward, I felt the intense drive to be worthy of that award. That was (somehow???) decades ago, and I still take out that piece of pumpkin-orange paper every now and then, smooth out the creases, and let the feelings from that day fill me again—the day eleven-year-old Renee felt the calling on her life to become an author and decided she would prove herself worthy of it.

My understanding of what it means to walk worthy of that calling on my life has changed over the years. I've often wished that the Poe Award came with a list of things I could do or ways I could behave that would instantly show I was walking worthy as a writer...that I was fulfilling my calling well.

But while that may not be the case for my calling as a writer—I just gotta figure it out as I go!—I have another calling on my life that I am beyond equipped for. And SO DO YOU!

All Christians have a calling within the Body of Christ as members in particular, as brothers and sisters bound together by Jesus, our peace. We are called to embrace and express the love of God to the world. We are called to be living epistles and examples to the lost. And we are given a snapshot of how to do it, too!

> **Ephesians 4:1-6**
> Therefore I, the prisoner of the Lord, urge you to walk in a manner worthy of the calling with which you were called, with all humility and meekness, with patience, bearing with one another in love, ³being diligent to keep the unity of the spirit in the bond of peace. ⁴*There is* one body and one spirit, just as also you were called in one hope of your calling, ⁵one Lord, one faith, one baptism, ⁶one God and Father of all, who is over all and through all and in all.

Because we have been given a noble calling, the highest commission in the world, we are also bidden to conduct ourselves in a way that is a credit to it.

Our demeanor with one another and with those around us is part of our living testimony. When we treat one another with the love of Christ—with humility, meekness, patience, and so on—we are accurately representing Jesus.

And it is then that we are truly walking in a manner worthy of our calling, in a way that exalts God and proves that we are His!

This Week's Prayer: Yahweh, thank You for placing a wonderful calling on my life in service to You! Please strengthen and empower me to walk worthy of it, day by day! Amen.

WHAT THE BODY DOES TO ITSELF

WOULDN'T IT BE AWESOME IF we could pick and choose what parts of our body are affected by the things we consume or what we do? Like if we could indulge in junk food that just affected our tastebuds, not our metabolic processes. Or if running could just burn in our legs, but not make our lungs ache or give us cramps, which are MUCH more uncomfortable!

Unfortunately, the things we do and what we consume have a much more widespread effect than just on the parts we wish they would.

The same is true for the Body of Christ, of which we are all members.

Ephesians 4:25 tells us that, "putting away falsehood, **each one is to speak the truth with his neighbor**, because we are members of one another." *The Message* version expands on this concept by saying that "in Christ's body we're all connected to each other, after all. When you lie to others, you end up lying to yourself."

It can be so easy to isolate our perception of ourselves within the Body of Christ—to say that what the hand does will not have any effect on the foot, since they're so far apart, or called to such different things. But we are all one Body, under one Head. When we conduct ourselves poorly with someone, it not only affects the other person, it affects us as well, and those connected to us.

Think about this: what is the actual sensation of pain? One medical article describes it this way: "Pain is felt when special nerves that detect tissue damage send signals to transmit information about the damage along the spinal cord to the brain. [...] The brain then decides what to do about the pain."

So, within the Body of Christ, pain among the members transmits up to the brain. To the head. To *Christ*. Therefore, if the Body cuts itself down, can it do so without harming the Body as a whole? And can it even feel the pain of harming itself without that pain going directly to the Head—which is *Christ*?

When division is sown within the Body, when we wound ourselves and the other members, when we pull the Body in all different directions, this pain is not only felt by the immediate people associated with the issue. It has a ripple effect, and one of those effects is the pain it causes Christ, as the Head. Our pain transmits to him.

There will always be pain caused to the Body. Some of it will not be within our control. But we are specifically called to speak the truth with each other because we are members of one another. We are joined, linked together by sinew and muscle and bone and tissue. The pain of our brothers and sisters, our fellow members, is *our* pain. And when we cause harm to one another, we cause harm to ourselves, to those around us, and to Jesus.

So as much as it is in our power, let's keep the connectivity forefront in our hearts and minds. Let's be mindful of the Body we share with all other

Christians. And let's do our best not to grieve the holy spirit of God, or to wound Christ with our behavior. And let's speak the truth in love to one another, so that our words and actions are healing and helpful, not harmful, to this Body of which we are *all* members in particular.

This Week's Prayer: Yahweh, thank You for this fascinating, beautiful Body of which You've made us all a part! Please help me to conduct myself in a way that cares for and honors Your Body and its head, Jesus! Amen.

TO THE PRAISE OF GOD'S GLORY

MORE THAN A FEW CHRISTIANS I've talked to over the years have struggled with understanding just what is truly asked of us when we're called to "praise" or "worship" God.

When the Bible tells us we'll be worshiping God to the ages of the ages, does that mean just one giant concert in Heaven?

Is praise an aspect of prayer?

What do those words even really mean?

For now, I want to focus on what praise is. Merriam-Webster's dictionary defines "praise" as "to express favorable judgment of [something]; to glorify, especially by the attributes of perfection."

So when we praise God, what we're doing is giving glory to Him, and especially to His attributes of perfection! This is certainly something that can be done in song and in prayer, but there's another aspect that's wrapped up not just in our words of praise, but in our very way of being.

We can praise with our lips all day long, and that does honor God; but are we praising Him with how we live our lives as well?

The Book of Ephesians speaks several times of things being "to the praise of God's glory." One of the things it addresses is *us*! WE are to be to the praise of God's glory—not just to praise Him with our lips, but to make our choices, our behavior, and our everyday life a source of praise to Him.

This means that we offer praise to God with our conduct, not just our words.

And more than that! We can be a reason that other people praise our Father in Heaven, too. The manner in which we walk out our lives can reflect on the glory of the One who created us and act as His provision for others in unfathomable ways!

So, while we make an effort to better praise God with our mouths, let's also measure our walk with Him and do our best to ensure that we are living our lives to the praise of God's glory.

This Week's Prayer: God, I praise You for all You are and all You have done! Help me to also praise You in the way I conduct my life, so that everything I do and all I am can be to the praise of Your glory! Amen.

ONCE DARKNESS, NOW LIGHT

FOR MOST CHRISTIANS, IT IS no secret that our lives began in darkness and will end in light.

While there are those, like myself, who have been born again for so long and from such an early time in life that we don't really comprehend a time before we lived in the light of Christ's redeeming sacrifice, there are others for whom that reality is much nearer and more vivid. They can picture what that darkness was like much more clearly, and in some cases, more painfully. And many remember the moment they escaped from it much more clearly, too.

Regardless of what we remember of that transitory moment in our lives, when it happened, it happened the same to all of us: in the instant we gave our lives to Christ, we were changed, we were washed in the cleansing blood of the Lamb, and we stepped from darkness to light.

But it was also much more than that.

God does not merely say we were *in* darkness during that time in our lives. In Ephesians 5:8, we're told that we *were darkness*. Now we *are light*. The powerful phrasal structure of this verse drives home a fact that is inferred in many places across Scripture: when we were ransomed from bondage and death by our acceptance of Christ's sacrifice on our behalf, our very *nature* changed.

When we first believed, we were changed from creatures of darkness, dead things puppeted by Death, to creatures of light, led by the Good Shepherd. Now we are called to walk as children of the light, bearing the fruit of righteousness, goodness, and truth. This is so different from the shameful and unfruitful works done by the children of darkness—the children we once were.

At times it can be difficult to grasp the magnitude of the shift that took place when we professed Christ as Lord. We may struggle to put to words how intense the battle against the forces of darkness became within us, because our nature became light, and light exposes the darkness that still lurks inside.

We were darkness itself. Now we are light, made in the image of the Father of Lights. And here we are, with a different nature, a different state of being from the inside out. And as children of the light, we must walk in that light, letting it shine before others so that they will see the fruitful works of goodness, righteousness, and truth, and glorify our Father who is in Heaven, and our savior Jesus who spilled his very blood to ransom us from darkness to that light.

This Week's Prayer: Yahweh, thank You for transforming my very essence from darkness to light! Please help me to live in a way that shines that light to all who see me—so that they see You. Amen.

PUT ON THE ARMOR

THERE IS SO MUCH EMPHASIS placed on the biblical charge to rid ourselves daily of the "old man" sin nature that was once our garment and put on the heavenly attire of the "new man" nature in Christ.

But there's actually a second "put on" command, just as imperative as the first: "Finally...Put on the whole armor of God." (Eph 6:10-11)

Why "finally"? Because we have to do the other putting off/putting on first! The armor won't fit us right or protect us well if what's beneath it is still rotten old bones. There's no sense in strapping defenses onto a dead body. But once we've stepped from darkness to light and embraced our reborn nature in Christ, now we have something worth protecting—and protect it we must!

This life is going to be a fight. And we must go into it equipped and outfitted to do battle.

Think about it this way: the enemy has very little to gain or lose in fighting an army of the dead. It's when we're alive and active in Christ that there's something—for him—worth attacking; and for us, there's something worth protecting.

So once we put on the new man nature, now we absolutely *have to step up and fight for what we have,* because the enemy will most definitely be lobbing a barrage of fiery arrows to incapacitate us.

Now we have risen from our state of living death; now we are putting off the old and putting on the new; now we are a growing threat to the enemy as we walk in the power of the holy spirit.

Now we must meet the challenge as overcomers.

It is imperative for all of us that we don't stop at putting on the new nature, leaving ourselves then susceptible to the attacks of the wicked one. We must take the next step and outfit ourselves with the armor of God so that we can not only transform—but then endure.

This Week's Prayer: Yahweh, thank You for equipping me with every bit of armor I need in this spiritual fight. Please help me stand strong for You and continue to use this armor as You intended. Amen.

BELTED WITH TRUTH

MY HUSBAND IS THE MASTER of the work aesthetic. He always makes sure he's dressed for success, no matter what the task is. I've always admired how put-together he is for the occasion, from hat to shoes to belt. Always gotta remember the belt! And he's right about that, because it's important that he has one—without it, his entire work ensemble doesn't stay on quite right.

I think it's no coincidence that the list of the armor of God begins with the belt. It's the part that holds the whole outfit together—and this was as true of ancient armor as it is today.

There were two roles the belt played in the Roman soldier's armor that I want to pay special attention to. One was that the belt was the support of the entire armor. It was often hung with leather strips that helped protect the lower extremities, and it secured all the other pieces of the armor.

The belt also held the scabbard, where the sword hung. With no belt, there was no sword.

Think about that for a moment. The belt and the sword went hand-in-hand. You needed to have your belt about you to carry your sword effectively into battle. The same is true for us: our starting place, the thing that secures all the rest of our armor, is the truth. It's the core element of our defense from the enemy's schemes.

And this is not truth as in "perfect doctrine," by the way—none of us will have absolutely perfect doctrine in this life. Rather, it's the truth of God's nature, of His promises, of Christ's purpose and power, and of our identity in Christ. It's God's plan, His purpose of the ages.

And how powerful are we, how much *more* powerful can we become in the spiritual battle, if we gird ourselves with that truth? If it protects our vital spots, if it's the security around which we fasten everything else?

All of this truth is contained within Scripture; but if the prospect of reading the entire Bible is a bit daunting to you, start with the Book of Ephesians, which encapsulates God's plan in a succinct way.

Take time to really deeply read through Ephesians from cover to cover. Do it several times, in several different versions. Soak up and sit in the truths it contains—about who we are, what we are called to, what is promised to us, what was done for us, and what we are to do for God. Let the truth in this story of God's purpose for the ages really live for you.

Then, take the time to branch out to other books of the Bible—the rest of the New Testament. Psalms and Proverbs. Invest in study tools to help you understand the parts that mystify you. Put forth the effort to deeply understand the truth contained throughout God's Word.

After all, it is not until we are properly armored that we can stand. And the truths we read from Scripture are what will keep our entire spiritual ensemble from falling apart.

Lash on the truth.

This Week's Prayer: Yahweh, thank You for the truth that helps gird me up and strengthens me for battle! Please help me to continuously reinforce myself with the truth of Your word. Amen.

PLATED WITH RIGHTEOUSNESS

NO MATTER HOW TOUGH WE try to be, underneath, we are all soft, squishy people.

Roman soldiers, though renowned and feared around much of the conquered world at the time of the Roman Empire, were no exception; so a vital part of their armor was the breastplate, which covered the torso and protected the squishiest bits we all have: the vital organs.

We also have a spiritual breastplate—one of righteousness. This piece of armor is crafted from two different kinds of righteousness: right living, and the righteousness inferred on us by the blood of Christ covering our sins. And we must have elements of *both* in our breastplate of righteousness, or else we leave different parts of ourselves exposed.

When we neglect the righteousness inferred by the blood of Christ and instead choose to dwell on our sins or our own works, we become vulnerable to blows of shame and guilt that cripple us to our innermost being.

When we neglect the righteousness of right living, we expose ourselves to egregious consequences both spiritual and physical. Unrestrained behavior and living in sin of any kind—consumptive, sexual, spiritual, etc.—leaves us vulnerable to attacks of every sort that can pierce our softest parts.

An added danger in both of these is that when we neglect one, we tend to eventually neglect the other. Those victimized by shame often turn to vices to numb the fiery darts that have pierced their hearts, which then leads to more shame, which leads to more numbing, and on and on.

We must belt our breastplate of righteousness to us with the truth of our place with Christ, our sins forgiven, our souls washed white as snow; and the truth of our duty to honor him as our Lord through upright and exemplary living.

When we are aware of the righteousness that protects our softest parts, and when we allow Christ's sacrifice to spur us on to a more righteous way of life, we are better protected against the enemy's attacks—and better able to stand firmly for God.

Lash on the truth. Strap on the righteousness.

This Week's Prayer: Yahweh, thank You for Your righteousness that helps guide and guard my heart! Please help me to stay in step with You and live fully in the righteousness You impart. Amen.

SHOD WITH READINESS

IT'S A SOUND WE ALL know well: the crash, the musical tinkling of shattering glass, the "Uh, oh" or occasionally more strongly-worded exclamation that follows.

Right around the time my son turned a year old, things started breaking. I know what you're probably thinking, but it genuinely wasn't his fault. It just happened that over the course of a few months after his first birthday:

- A glass-topped end-table shattered (okay, that one WAS him)
- A latte maker exploded mid-brew
- A baking dish randomly fell off the top of the fridge

Thankfully, he wasn't hurt despite an alarming proximity to these incidences. But that didn't stop me from going over the floor with a magnifying glass afterward, ensuring there were no tiny glass slivers waiting to dig into his tender little feet. And for a little bit afterward each time, we were wearing extra thick socks or shoes in the house, just in case.

When there's something sharp or otherwise dangerous on the floor, it's instinctive that we go for something tough enough to protect our feet. The same was true of a Roman soldier's footwear; you wouldn't really imagine a man in armor running barefoot into battle! And they didn't; their shoes helped protect them from being crippled by anything from a sharp stone to the sole, to a dead enemy's weapon that could slice the tendons of the foot apart in one sweep. Good footwear allowed them both to move quickly and to stand firm in any circumstances, because their shoes were made out of the right stuff for the fight.

We have this protection, too. Our feet are shod with readiness brought about through peace.

"Peace" may not sound all that strong, in a sense. But preparing ourselves for the battle by cultivating peace with God and with ourselves, and making peace with the dangers and challenges that will come before we even face them, allows us to be tough no matter what.

The readiness we must adapt into our armor in the spiritual battle has its source in knowing the Good News of peace—of *our* peace, Jesus Christ.

When we outfit ourselves with peace, we accept that we are in it for the long haul.

We accept that we will face difficult times, trials, and adversities of every sort.

We are prepared to stand firm on the battlefield and face any onslaught because we have come to the battle with the right attitude and attire.

We have found an inner stillness, a peace with God and within ourselves so that we are ready for whatever the enemy sends our way.

And when we have the right footwear—when we come to the fight prepared, bring that readiness of peace with us, square up and dig our heels in—we will be able to stand against the enemy's charge.

Lash on the truth. Strap on the righteousness. Plant your feet.

This Week's Prayer: Yahweh, thank You for the readiness to stand! Please help me remain peaceful so I'm not swayed from my stance on Your truth. Amen.

27

SHIELDED IN TRUST

FROM A FAIRLY YOUNG AGE, one of my favorite movies was *Braveheart.* I remember sitting in rapt attention on the living room floor, stuffed horse gripped to my chest, watching the scene when the Scotsmen taunted their English enemies and then promptly retreated from the reciprocating storm of arrows behind a shell of wooden shields.

Ever since I first saw that movie, shields have fascinated me. I've researched all different kinds for different writing projects, and one thing that's really struck me is how much thought goes into crafting a shield. It's more than just a wood or metal blocker. Not only does a shield protect, it can also deflect a blow, snag an enemy's weapon and disarm him, or even be used to deal damage itself.

The shield is versatile—just like the power of our trust in God.

Having firm trust helps protect us from the blows the enemy brings in the spiritual war; it provides the defense in knowing that as we lean on God during times of assault, these blows will not be our end. Our trust also helps us to disarm the enemy: to remove the power of those blows straight from his vicious hands.

And our trust allows us to step forward and take back lost ground, confident in the God of angel armies standing at our back.

Making certain our shield is strong—that our trust in God is secure, given the proper attention, reinforced when it weakens, built back up if the blows leave it more fragile than it ought to be—is not only crucial to our protection and survival on this battlefield; it's important for those around us, too.

In times of ancient warfare, it was common for the warriors of some armies, like the Greeks and Romans, to sport shields that protected more than just the single soldier.

The shields were large enough or otherwise carefully designed to provide protection for the sheildbearer and at least one of his fellow warriors. And in the case of a fighting force working together, like the Scotsmen in *Braveheart* or Leonidas's men in *300*, the shields could all close in like a shell, helping protect everyone's flanks at once.

That is what the shield of our trust does. It not only helps us defend against the fiery arrows of the wicked one, to disarm and fight back...it can also help protect those who are close by. Our act of trust becomes their defense, their teacher, their rallying sign. It can help give them the courage to raise their shields, too, and protect those around *them*.

The shield of trust is the first piece of the armor of God that we don't wear. We *carry* it. So we must make the choice to keep lifting it even when it grows heavy...even when we feel we lack the strength. We must find a way to step forward into our trust, again and again, for the protection of ourselves and those around us.

Lash on the truth. Strap on the righteousness. Plant your feet. Raise your shield.

This Week's Prayer: Yahweh, thank You for the shield You equip us with to help protect us in the spiritual battle. Help me to be strong in trust, to lift it, and to use it well in defense of myself and others. Amen.

HELMED IN SALVATION

THERE ARE A LOT OF things we can live without, but we can't live without a head.

Unless you're fighting a hydra, the general consensus in battle is that the head is a pretty good target to aim for. It's one of the surest ways to incapacitate your opponent. You don't even have to knock their head clean off—just a good hard blow can be enough to put someone out of commission.

Warriors have known this for centuries, and that's why a headguard or helmet of some fashion has been a staple of armor sets for armies across empires, regimes, kingdoms, and dynasties for thousands of years. Every warrior knows the crippling power of a blow to the head.

This is true both physically and in the mental sense; when we take a blow to the head in the spiritual fight, it can take us down for far too long. While we struggle to shake the stars from our eyes and stand back up, precious ground could be lost. Or we could sustain worse injuries while we're too weak to defend ourselves.

Make no mistake—the enemy knows this. Head-blows are one of his cruel specialties. He will do everything in his capacity to catch you without a helmet on and land a blow that will render you incapacitated in the fight. And one of the strongest weapons in his arsenal is the kind of doubt that rattles our heads so much, we take *ourselves* out of the fight.

This is why the helmet of salvation is more crucial than any headguard in any armor set that's ever been made by mortal hands.

We are never more protected than when we understand the truth of our salvation.

This is a simple fact rooted in the truth that, when we know the power we have through accepting Jesus as our Lord and Savior, and when we know the future that's promised to us, it takes power out of the enemy's swings.

Sure, he can land a few blows here and there, but in the grand scheme of things, they lose their vigor.

What's a knock to the skull next to eternal life?

What's a nasty threat or a harsh lie when we have the power of holy spirit within us?

What is he? What *is* he next to the glory of all that God is, all that He has been, all He will continue to be?

The helmet of salvation guards our minds and allows us to see the battle for what it is: not our end, but our on-the-way. Not our everything, but our for-now.

And no matter how bloody and difficult the trenches get, through the sacrifice of Christ we are promised to see the other side.

Knowing the saving power of our God and the hope of our redeemed future allows us to keep our minds sharp, focused, and ready for the fight, not distracted by the troubles and tribulations of this life.

Lash on the truth. Strap on the righteousness. Plant your feet. Raise your shield. Fasten your helmet.

This Week's Prayer: Yahweh, thank You for the incredible gift of SALVATION! Thank you for the eternal life You grant through belief in Your Son. Help me to continuously guard my mind with the knowledge that my life and future are secure in You. Amen.

ARMED WITH THE SPIRIT'S SWORD

I GREW UP AROUND WEAPONS. My brother and I were raised to respect them. I remember being taught over and over again that if you're going to pick up a weapon, you'd better hold it carefully and be aware of what it can do, so you can use it well.

The antithesis of this knowledge, of course, was a principle we also were heavily taught: if you do not use your weapon well, you can hurt people you don't intend to.

The Sword of the Spirit—the Word of God—is the primary offensive weapon in this struggle against the rulers, authorities, principalities, and powers of darkness in the spiritual realms.

If we do not take up this sword, we're well-armored but ineffective moving targets. In the spiritual battle, it's not enough to be outfitted; we must be *equipped* and willing to go on the offensive.

The sword most often used by the Roman soldier was the gladius, a havoc-wreaking weapon with the ability to pierce even the strongest enemy armor.

In the same way, the Sword that belongs to the Spirit—God, His very Word given to us—is a powerful weapon in the spiritual realm. It allows us to separate good from evil by the measured balance of God's razor-edged standard. It divides to the very marrow of the bones, to the thoughts and intentions of the heart.

It is also a weapon that is used in the mortal realm, and that's one of the reasons it's crucial that we respect it and hold it carefully.

Many terrible things have been done in the name of God by people who thought they were wielding this sword accurately; but it has been a deep cut that has bled on the world itself, and it has even pierced the very Body of Christ.

This sword is not to be wielded with a riled and reckless hand against Christ's Body or against other people; it must be understood and respected so that it's not brandished amiss.

We are God's soldiers, fighting in His army, and we have a duty to discern the truth through His Word and then act accordingly.

The Sword of the Spirit is a weapon alive and powerful, capable of defense and attack; it is always sharp, always balanced, always battle-ready. And we must learn to draw it and put it to use in a way that honors the one who bestowed it on us.

When we have all the pieces of this armor put together—when our minds and soft spots are protected, our feet strong, our sword and shield in hand, and it's all held together by the truth of God and Christ and our identity in them, and what we are fighting for—we have finally done the putting on.

We have picked up the sword. We have entered the fight.

This is what God has called us to do. We must stand for Him. We must fight in His name. And we must do it in a way that honors and glorifies our Great Father.

So lash on the truth. Strap on the righteousness. Plant your feet. Raise your shield. Fasten your helmet. Ready your sword.

And STAND.

This Week's Prayer: Yahweh, thank You for the Word that is our weapon in the spiritual war! Help me wield it honorably, skillfully, and as You see fit. Amen.

ON GOD'S TEAM

THERE'S A VERSE IN EPHESIANS THAT that used to confuse me as a kid. It talks about how God "chose us in him before the foundation of the world to be holy and without blemish in his presence in love" (Eph. 1:4). I wasn't raised in the Calvinistic viewpoint that God predestined individuals to be saved, but I also didn't know how this verse fit into the scope of free will. If not *individuals*, who did God choose before the foundation of the world, exactly?

The elucidation of this verse finally came in my late teens through an analogy about basketball: if someone decides to form a basketball team for a college, they prepare the court, the facilities, even the team name before a single player is selected. Then individuals try out for the team.

Think about that in light of Ephesians 1:4. Long before you or I or anyone else existed, God was pulling together a team. He knew this team would face a lot of persecution and controversy throughout its existence. He knew the "game" would be hard; blood, sweat, and tears would mar the court He was planning to build. But He assigned us an amazing coach, one who was tempted in every way as we are, who leads this team on a sure charge to victory.

Now it's up to us as individuals to decide if we're going to try out for the team.

The amazing thing? You're guaranteed a spot on the roster as long as you confess Jesus as your Lord and Savior and believe God raised him from the dead. And God *invites* everyone to join, to play their best for Him, to get skin in the game because we HAVE skin in the game. There's no room for sideline benchwarmers here, and in the game of life on God's court there aren't even plain spectators.

We want as many people playing on our side as possible because there are really only two sides, and our coach says "Anyone who isn't with me opposes me, and anyone who isn't working with me is actually working against me." (Luke 11:23)

The stakes could be no higher and the reward no greater. This is not some gilded trophy we're striving for, but the prize of eternal life. And the souls of those not yet on this team are at stake.

Before the very base of the world was laid, God always intended for there to be a team, and it is up to the individual to choose if they will partake and recruit others to join up.

Are you in?

This Week's Prayer: Yahweh, thank You for reserving a place for all of us on Your team! Help me to play to my strengths for You, to take the game seriously and recruit as many as possible to Your team! Amen.

HOW TO BE AN IMITATOR OF GOD

EPHESIANS 5 STARTS OUT WITH a pretty hefty commission: to be imitators of God.

You know. *YAHWEH GOD.* The all-powerful, perfect Being Who created the universe, Who parts seas and keeps burning bushes alive, Who raises the dead and forgives sins, Who is always fair and just, slow to anger and abounding in love.

That God.

Seems like a pretty tall order to start with! And not only that, we must *also* be like Jesus, who walked in great faith and love, living a sinless life and then enduring unimaginable suffering on the cross for the redemption of all mankind.

No pressure!

But I absolutely love the perspective *The Message* version brings to these opening verses in Ephesians 5. It so beautifully weaves in angles of childlike adoration, achievable goals despite our sinful state, and the power of godly love that changes not only our lives, but the lives of those we show it to:

"Watch what God does, and then you do it, like children who learn proper behavior from their parents. Mostly what God does is love you. Keep company with him and learn a life of love. Observe how Christ loved us. His love was not cautious but extravagant. He didn't love in order to get something from us but to give everything of himself to us. Love like that."

When I read this passage, I realize I don't have to be perfect to do God's will or imitate Him. I need to model myself after His way of being, certainly—but that's not something I can do stumbling around in the dark, guessing all over the place! And these verses give us a great perspective on where to start.

I need to keep company with God—in prayer, praise, and reading His Word. I need to watch how God was and *is* with people and make that my way of being, just like I learned compassion and ministering from my earthly parents. I need to be open to learning—which means being open to correction!

Observe how Christ loved us? I can do that! Not only in my personal life and the testimony of others, but the Gospels are also some of my favorite records in the Bible. Love selflessly and extravagantly—that's exactly what I want to do! And I want Jesus to teach me to do it better, every day!

Being imitators of God and Jesus can seem like a daunting task at times. But when we break it down to the meaty center, it's really about being in relationship with them intimately enough that we learn how to live a life of love and sacrifice, of putting others first, of thinking of ourselves less and others more. We learn to imitate God by being in relationship with Him; we learn to imitate Christ by studying how he loved, and walking in his footsteps.

It's a relational charge. An intimate one. It's our call to love and action.

This Week's Prayer: Yahweh, thank You for being the perfect, wonderful, loving example in Whose image I was made! Please help me to imitate You and Your Son in love, in word and in deed, to draw people closer to You and to live my life as best I can. Amen.

IN ALL THINGS, SEEK HIM FIRST

WHEN TROUBLE COMES OR YOU find yourself in need, how quickly does your heart turn to God? How close is He to the forefront of your thoughts? Is your instinct to turn to people for help, or to Him?

There are lots of reasons why we may not think to turn to God first. One can be plain old habit; another can be the "immediacy" of affirmation from those around us when we share our concerns with them.

For my part, I struggled for a long time with the fear that if I prayed for something and it didn't happen—especially when I thought I was praying within the will of God—that it somehow meant either He didn't love me, or worse, that maybe He just didn't listen to prayers at all.

But what a limiting worldview! I had completely forgotten where Ephesians 3 tells us of **"Him who is able to do far more abundantly than all that we ask or think, according to the power at work in us..."** and instead I was "deciding" well before the fact that God wouldn't care to act on my behalf, that He would not give in abundance in my time of need. So why even bother?

This created such a coldness in my spirit, a sense that what I thought was important and what was important to God were two very different things. It took me years to fathom this callousness around my heart and begin to chisel away at it.

So how do we go about prioritizing our reliance on God? How do we make the shift to seeking Him first in all things?

For me, it's taken conscious effort. I teach this lesson to others now as often as I can—verbally and through written words like these!—so they'll stick in *my* brain, too. When troubles arise, I have to mentally slam on the brakes and ask myself, "Have I talked to God about this yet?" Then I carve out time to pour my heart out to Him.

It's a process, let me tell ya. I still have moments where my first instinct is to consult my friends before my Father. Thankfully, He is patient with me—and because I've asked, He's been faithful to bring this lesson to remembrance as often as I need it.

So now I pray He brings it to YOUR remembrance, too: His nearness, the abundance of His love, the greatness of what He can do, and the peace and inspiration that comes with seeking Him first in all things great and small.

This Week's Prayer: Yahweh, thank You for acting so powerfully and abundantly in Your love for us! Please help me to always be mindful as I pray and live out my life that I can and must rely on You for all things! Amen.

HOW TO ACHIEVE TRUE HUMILITY

I FIND MYSELF REFLECTING OFTEN on the things the Apostle Paul said about himself. Despite the great good he did to spread the Good News, he referred to himself in such glowing terms as "chief among sinners" (1 Tim.) and "least of all the holy ones" (Eph. 3). No one could accuse Paul of resting on his own laurels! Instead of boasting about his achievements, he chose to boast about the accomplishments of his peers in Jesus, and of course in the wondrous works of the Lord.

Reading Paul's epistles has brought me face-to-face with the sharp contrast between true and false humility. Sometimes pride masquerades itself as humility through self-deprecation, which seeks to be told it's good enough. In other words, think of the "pious humility" of one who might claim to be a terrible sinner, a mess-up, just the worst, but what they're really hoping for is someone to tell them they aren't really that bad after all.3

True humility, on the other hand, is the understanding of the human condition. It's the recognition of the truth in passages like Ephesians 2, which speaks of the dead state we all came from. It's a genuine, unmitigated face-to-face confrontation with our very nature that allows us to realize we are broken, flawed, powerless on our own, and that it's only through Christ that we have enough. That we ARE enough.

Of all the bad things he did before Jesus reached his heart, Paul was not unaware. Rather than boasting in his own strength, in the things he endured and survived, he boasted in Christ through whom he had a second chance and the opportunity to be part of something greater.

One of my mentors liked to use the phrase "none of us deserves to be here" in reference to the Body of Christ...and it's true. We are saved by grace, not works. Understanding that we didn't receive our glorious salvation of ourselves, but by the gift of God, brings us face-to-face with just how broken we are without Him.

Once we cease to rely on our singular strength, once we stop falling back on the support of our own merit—as if that could ever be enough to carry us through—we open our hearts to the humbleness that allows us to be true vessels of God and Christ.

But in order to be good witnesses for them, we can't be witnesses of ourselves. We must start from a place of true humility.

This Week's Prayer: Yahweh, thank You for being my strength! Thank You for saving me by Your grace from all my brokenness. Help me to always be humble and live in surrender to Your wonderful love. Amen.

WHAT SONG HAS GOD PLACED IN YOUR HEART?

MUSIC IS ONE OF MY favorite things in life. Before I became a mom, I probably listened to a good 5 hours of music at least every day!

I like to think I come very honestly by my love of music. My entire family is musical, though in my case, not musically *talented*, just musically *inclined*. As a kid, I remember the tug-of-war my brother and I would play for who got to choose the music on cleaning days (since I did not yet have the magical ability to put in headphones and listen to my OWN tunes). This was a huge point of contention because our tastes are—and have always been—so different! Yet our passion for music is equal in every way.

I find myself drawn often to the verse in Ephesians 4 that talks about the different functions God has called people to: apostles, prophets, pastors, evangelists, teachers. You only need to set foot in a Christian congregation to know the gifts there are as diverse as the people themselves!

Like a favorite song, we each have a gift placed in us that is unique. It is no more or less valid or important than anyone else's. My brother may not love every song I love, but does that make *my* love for that song any less valid? Not at all!

Just the same, Christ's Body thrives on diversity. Your unique gift—the song YOU sing in the great harmony of God's story—is indispensable! And I encourage you to embrace that!

Seek out God's heart for how to make the most of your ministry and sing YOUR song to the praise of His Glory!

This Week's Prayer: Yahweh, thank You for equipping Your Body with different functions that make us all so unique! Help me to know my function fully—to sing my song well to edify You and others. Amen.

THE PERSONAL REDEEMER

WHAT A POWERFUL THING IT IS to be children of the One who redeemed all mankind through the sacrifice of His Son. The One who reaped us back from death, Who does more abundantly for us than we could ever even think to ask.

And how often do we neglect to ask? How often do we try to put brokenness back together with our own hands?

What broken pieces have scarred your hands that you should have given up to Him? And why? Is it guilt? Shame? Stubbornness? Pride? What is keeping you from giving these things to the Redeemer?

Consider deeply.

What have you committed to the Lord that you feel you've fallen short in or fallen away from?

Is there an area of your life you dedicated to Him, only to lose your focus later?

Are you like Simon Peter? What are the waves around you? Have you asked Jesus to quiet those storming waters?

Our God is a God of second chances—and third chances, and fourth chances. Oh, so many chances. He is invested in us. In our success. In teaching and training us to trust Him and turn to Him in all things.

What did you once hold precious and true that you now feel is lost?

Did you know God can redeem it all? Every last thing that you've given up, He can redeem—He can make beauty from ashes, a life-changing lesson from a mistake. He heals the broken-hearted and rebuilds from absolute ruin.

There is no need for shame. Conviction, certainly! Do not let self-degradation keep you from coming to the healer of nations.

Bring your brokenness and your sorrow and the things you've given up to Him. And let the Redeemer redeem.

This Week's Prayer: Yahweh, thank You for Your redeeming love! Thank You for everything You and Your Son gave to make us family. Help me to lay aside all pride and shame so that I can come before You and find redemption. Amen.

HOW TO CHANGE THE WORLD
IN 5 STEPS

SO, YOU WANT TO CHANGE THE WORLD?

AWESOME! Me, too! I think we should all want to do this, considering the power of the truth we carry and the great commission to make disciples of all nations! Difficult to do that without changing *some* things, right?

But where to even start? When you have all this knowledge and all these people to reach with it, what's the first move?

Well, that's what this chapter is here to help you with! In just five steps, you can change the world and reach countless people with the Good News!

Ready? Here's how you do it!

1. Love the Lord Your God with All Your Heart, Soul, Mind & Strength
2. Love Your Neighbor as Yourself
3. Love Your Spouse
4. Love Your Children
5. Treat Others As You Want to be Treated

Go back and read that list.

Cool, now reread it.

I never said they were easy steps! Neither did Jesus when he commissioned us to do them.

But while we may never change the world the way Jesus himself did—after all, we aren't the fulcrum of history, if history even remembers us in a few centuries—there is undeniable power in living the love of Christ to the person next to you. To the people under your roof. In putting God first and treating others with the love of Jesus.

Changing the world doesn't always happen with a splash. It's ripple after ripple as we cast out the stones of love. If you're the only person to treat someone else with godly love, you may be the reason they're inspired to treat their spouse with love, which may be the reason that spouse does something kind for their children, who do loving acts for a friend at school—

Do you want to change the world? Love as Jesus loved, not as the world loves. Tear down walls. Unite, don't divide. Invest in God and people with your whole heart.

That's how you change the world. It's that simple. It's that difficult.

It's that powerful.

This Week's Prayer: Yahweh, thank You for the small and powerful ways we can change this world. Thank You that in everything we do and everything we are, we have the chance to represent You. Help me to change the world through the love of Your Son. Amen.

WHAT'S IN YOUR BACKPACK?

A FRIEND ONCE TOLD ME a story of two Buddhist monks walking down the road. They reached a river along the way and found a wealthy woman searching for a way to cross without sullying her fine clothes.

Being celibate to the point of abstaining from all contact with women, the monks were convicted to pass her by; nevertheless, one of them picked the woman up, carried her across the river, set her down, and continued on his way with his companion.

After some time, the second monk turned to his friend and said, "As monks, we aren't permitted even to touch a woman. How could you carry that one on your shoulders?"

The other monk looked at him and replied, "Brother, I set her down on the other side of the river. Why are you still carrying her?"

This story really drove home for me how much it's in our nature to carry around things we should've left behind a long time ago.

Human brains are like sponges, capable of absorbing much, and often indiscriminate in what we soak up—the good and the bad.

To put it another way, we load our backpacks with rocks and try to keep a good pace moving down the road. We don't often pause to think of what we're still carrying with us that we should've left behind.

Take a look at your life. Open your backpack. What are you toting around that's weighing you down? Lift up your arms; what are you carrying that you should've put down at the riverside?

Though we are renewed and redeemed, many of us carry the broken pieces of our former selves in our backpack. We tote around our old man nature rather than putting him off entirely like we should.

We have great capacity to serve God even when struggling under heavy burdens. But how much more can we do for Him when we're thriving at capacity, unburdened by dead weight and things that we no longer need to carry with us?

What can you release that will allow you to become a better servant for the Lord?

This Week's Prayer: Yahweh, thank You for bringing to mind the burdens we carry that inhibit us from fully serving You! Help me empty my backpack of the weight that makes me less effective in bringing to pass Your purposes. Amen.

WHY IS OBEDIENCE IMPORTANT?

OBEDIENCE IS NO EASY LIFESTYLE.

Whether it's obedience to parents, workplace superiors, team leaders, or the ultimate authority—God Himself!—there's always a part of our spirit that will dig its heels in and defy.

A lot of times this reaction is driven by the sinful nature in us—that angry slice of our being that insists we know better, can do better, that *we* should be in charge and calling all the shots because we've got the wherewithal to be the absolute masters of our own destinies.

The problem with this way of thinking is that we will rarely find an area in life where we have ultimate knowledge about anything.

Never is this truer than as it pertains to God. We will never know more than Him, our wisdom about what we want and "need" cannot surpass His understanding about what is truly best for us. To insist on living in disobedience to Him because we think we know better is pridefully deceptive to ourselves and to those who are looking to us to model upright, authentic, integral Christian living.

Jesus said we show our love for him (and by extension, for the Father) when we keep his commandments. Living by our own set of rules shows love for one person and one only: ourselves.

We exemplify our dedication to self and our own comfort when we prioritize obedience to our own whims over obedience to God—even if obedience to Him causes discomfort.

Why does obedience cause discomfort, then, if He knows what's best for us?

Simple: because it chafes against that natural pride, that inherent self-seeking, the mentality that prizes one's personal, often passive and temporal happiness over eternal joy and security promised by the Father.

Obedience is important because it places our trust and actions behind the One who sees what we can't, the One who sees not just the momentary payoff but the full scope of what our actions bring about.

To live in harmony with His commands will always bring about what is ultimately the best result, even if in the moment it makes us unpopular, uncomfortable, or unhappy.

And that, above all, is what makes obedience so worthwhile.

This Week's Prayer: Yahweh, thank You for the free will choice to live in obedience to You! Please help me to always be mindful of why it's so important to obey You, so that I'm prepared to choose obedience even under the toughest circumstances. Amen.

WHY IS SURRENDER CHALLENGING?

AS A KID, I WENT to a lot of Christian conferences with long praise and worship sessions. But I didn't mind; I loved the high-energy dancing with my friends and singing at the top of my lungs in the community spirit with the whole room.

But there was always a part of worship that made me uncomfortable: when it got quiet and a lot of the adults would raise their hands, bow their heads, and even kneel.

I couldn't explain why that made me uncomfortable until much later in life, when I realized I've always had a bit of a control issue. I don't like surrendering to things. I don't like crying in front of people. I don't like not knowing what the plan is. I don't like being out of control. And even at a young age, the idea of surrendering so completely to God, *in front of people!*, was absolutely terrifying.

I learned in my teen years that I wasn't alone. At every youth camp I went to, there were a handful of my peers who I could tell *wanted* to raise their hands and sing out praises at the top of their lungs, but like me, they remained in the aisles, hands turned up at their sides, unwilling to show that level of surrender before God or their fellow teens.

Why is surrender difficult? Because at its core, surrender requires vulnerability. It's upturned palms and bowed heads and us on our knees. There are few positions more vulnerable than that, because on the knees, one is defenseless, unable to flee. You have to have absolute trust that you're not going to be attacked!

But surrender is not merely a posture we take during praise and worship; it's a posture of the *heart*. To be in complete surrender before God requires that everything we are—and aren't—every good and terrible part of us, lays vulnerable before Him. As if we could hide ourselves, anyway, like Adam and Eve in the garden...but there's still something *different* about surrender versus merely being seen.

Surrendering to God will deepen our relationship with Him beyond words, but it requires action from us. It isn't waiting for God to search us; it's bringing what we are to Him, all the good, the bad, and the ugly, knowing He will only bring about the best for us. We are safe with Him, every angle, every inch.

It is terrifying! It is tough! And it is life-changing. We will never experience more emotional or spiritual intimacy with our Creator than when we surrender ourselves, fully and completely, heart and soul, to Him.

This Week's Prayer: Yahweh, thank You for the opportunity to experience deep, intimate fellowship with You! Help me surrender my pride and any unease I feel so I can fully submit to, and fully experience, You! Amen.

LEARNING HOW GOD SPEAKS TO YOU

MY EXPERIENCE GROWING UP IN the faith was both an incredible privilege and a source of unique challenges.

I certainly had *plenty* of great, godly people to look up to, but from a very young age I was confused, uncertain, and a little let down that I couldn't seem to find a place where God taught me the kinds of lessons He doled out to others with such frequency and life-changing depth: prophets with visions, prophetesses with dreams; scriptural revelations pouring from the page, bringing fresh perspectives to the bewildered and setting the captives free; healings performed on our living room sofa; words of knowledge and revelation spoken with conviction.

These were all around me in my childhood, and my human nature tempted me deep into a place of self-deprecation when these experiences didn't happen to me.

I've spoken to so many people who, like me, see the spiritual experiences of others and wonder why God doesn't talk to them or work through them like that. And these are not typically people who want fame or recognition for being a vessel of God's holy spirit; more often, they crave the depth of intimacy that comes from experiencing the co-laborer relationship with their Heavenly Father. There's nothing like dancing that dance with Him. *Nothing*.

For many years, I did not think God spoke to me at *all*. Prophetic workshops and manifestations at fellowship always ended up a dry well for me. It wasn't until I was in my mid-twenties that I finally realized God *was* speaking to me—just not how He was speaking to my heroes of the faith.

God speaks to me through writing and through conversation. He does this in ways I have never seen Him do with anyone else—and that's not to say He *doesn't*, but I want to call attention to the fact that we can get so focused on wishing God would speak to us in one *particular* capacity that we miss the myriad other ways He actually *does*.

I once went through a struggle with a character in one of my novels; I'd spent a morning wrestling with her arc and finally gave up and stepped back. I knew I was missing something, and I was too fed-up to make it work! So I went to work and sat down to write blogs, but when trying to think through what I would say, God edged something else in there instead.

"Get ready," He said. "I'm about to teach you the next big lesson through her."

It's hard to explain the emotions I felt at that clear word: my first thought was "Uh oh, oh boy," because if God is going to give me a lesson to teach through a character, I'd better get it right! But quickly following on the heels of that was an overwhelming sense of excitement—and a warmth I can't even describe.

Because after years and years of wishing and hoping God would speak to me like He did the "spiritual heavy-hitters" in my life, I was finally figuring out how to be comfortable in my own ministry; to hear His voice and find His lessons in the places He gives them to me. Not through pictures or dreams, but through words and lessons on the page.

Look closely at your life. Forsaking all the ways you WISH God might speak to you, look for how He already *does*.

Are you an artist? Where are His lessons swirled among the watercolors, sketched in the lead, swept in the charcoal?

Are you a writer? Where do the words leap loud and vibrant off the page? Where does your mortal understanding suddenly become something *more*? Where did YOU learn a lesson as the letters dripped from your fingertips?

Are you a businesswoman? A realtor? A landscaper? A truck driver? What are you in the depths of your spirit? How is God speaking to you through the threads of passion and purpose that make up who *you* are?

Because I promise you, He *is* speaking to you. He knit you together in your mother's womb. You are fearfully and wonderfully made.

Every fiber of your being is a tapestry in which His wonderful power is woven; and through each of those precious threads, His voice is resonating, His lessons and love channeling along the immaculate craftsmanship of your very essence.

Seek, brothers and sisters. Seek with your whole heart, and you will find Him there.

This Week's Prayer: Yahweh, thank You for the unique and wonderful ways in which You communicate with me! Help me become sensitive to Your voice in all the areas of my life so I can follow Your leading in all I do. Amen.

YOUR PAST IS GOD'S GLORY

IT CAN BE ALL TOO easy to label ourselves as damaged goods. From things we've done or that have been done to us, many Christians or people considering giving their lives to Jesus stand on the slippery precipice of shame, a foot in the kingdom and another in the world, their souls just one aching thought or painful night away from utterly embracing the belief that they're of no use to God.

A life of crime. A battle with addiction. A spate of lovers. A misstep, a stumble, a dark road you turned down for too many years.

Now you feel filthy. Damaged. Broken. Placeless in God's plans and purposes.

One time a friend showed me the website of a pastor he met by coincidence on a flight (or so he thought). This was a woman covered in tattoos and piercings, laughing with pure joy on her face in the picture taken of her, attached to an article on her life's story. A bio piece in a magazine detailed her past of paganism and loose living and how finding Jesus changed everything for her.

Still decorated and pierced—not just her face now, but straight through the heart with Christ's love—she used her testimony to carry truth to people walking the same path she once did.

I thought about her picture as I looked at myself that day: unpierced, lightly-tattooed, and with a past of being raised in a Christian household with loving Christian parents.

Could my story reach the same kids and young adults she's reaching? Maybe.

I'm going to say probably not, though.

Now, my testimony is no less valid than hers, of course—none of ours is. But I couldn't help but think of how easy it could be to scorn this woman for her past. To think less of her because of her appearance or shun her for her history with ungodly practices.

As I was pondering all these things, God brought a notion that resonated through me like a bell rung in my spirit: "If you didn't have a past, some people might not have a future."

We often talk about God turning pain into joy, but somehow it can be much more difficult to grasp how He uses our past for His purposes. How He can use the testimony of a former lost sheep to bring others to the flock.

Those with the darkest, most painful history can often reach others in places just as dark—people who would not be reachable by those with what might be considered a more "conventional" past.

So my encouragement is this: don't let your past define you with shackles of shame. Don't let it keep you from serving and surrendering to God. Your past may be the guide for others to find a future in Christ.

Tell your story with fearless authenticity, surrendering all you were and all you are to your Heavenly Father. Let your scars draw maplines for the lost, straight to God.

The dividing wall is torn down. We need your testimony, your strength, your past to help others experience everlasting life in the Family of God.

This Week's Prayer: Yahweh, thank You for redeeming even the most difficult aspects of my life! Thank You that my story doesn't end in its darkest parts. Help me to use my testimony to bring new hearts to Your caring hands. Amen.

THE VALUE OF GRIT & PRESSURE

LIVING WITH DISCOMFORT IS...WELL, rather uncomfortable.

People often take great steps to avoid it. We flee from awkward situations, avoid difficult conversations, and bow out of tough social events. Parents do their best to keep their children from experiencing hurt, disappointment, and the sting of failure. Coworkers cover for each other. Friends hide grievances behind sad smiles.

But in all of this, we're only maintaining the status quo. We are not experiencing or encouraging the painful tearing that comes before the muscle grows. In hiding from pain and discomfort, we rob ourselves and/or others of the chance to become stronger.

Character is built by learning to grow graciously under pressure. Two of the most valuable ornamentations in this world—pearls and diamonds—cannot come to be without two distinct things: grit (pearls) and pressure (diamonds). Certainly, imitations of these priceless things can be made…but they prove easily-scuffed and far less durable than the real pearl or diamond that has gone through the grit or pressure to be fully formed.

People are not so different. In order to shine, in order to adorn the Body of Christ with our valuable glow, we are often not *hidden* from grit and pressure. We must go *through* them. Like the refiner's fire, these seasons of heat and discomfort birth stronger, sterner stuff within us. What is never taxed never strengthens—and what isn't strong will break.

But subject something to the wrong kind of pressure and it breaks anyway.

This is why God's brand of discipline is so important. It's the right kind of pressure that ensures we neither crack under the strain nor remain too soft to endure.

So when trying times come—as they will—rather than seeing them as waves to ride out or inconveniences to endure, seek diligently how you can *grow* from them. Try to discern how this can be your refiner's fire, how this crucible can make you stronger.

Look for how the grit and pressure can help shape you to shine for the Lord.

This Week's Prayer: Yahweh, thank You for Your discipline that refines and purifies me! Help me to always find ways to grow and improve through Your Word and instruction and those You send into my life. Amen.

THE WORLD IS OUR MISSION FIELD

I WROTE THESE WORDS FROM MY favorite coffeeshop. Not in my usual spot, which was taken up that morning by a meeting of college students; instead, I was tucked away on one of the older benches, facing the bar counter. Right before me hung a pair of chalkboards that told of the charitable organizations this shop gave its tips to.

I read the countries of outreach on one: Guatemala. Haiti. Honduras. India. The list went on.

Then I read the other: Local. Backpacks for kids. Boys and Girls club. Winter shelter for battered and homeless people. Midway houses. Flood relief—in my own state.

One of the reasons this coffeeshop was so popular in this college town (and remained that way for over a decade until its unfortunate, untimely closure in late 2020) was that it was active in its missions. The organization saw needs and tackled them. Strung across the walls were testimonies where this coffee shop had brought relief—and the love of Christ—to the hurting and hopeless around the world.

I don't know that we Christians ask ourselves often enough whether we're really serving the mission field God has called us to collectively or as individuals.

Are we content to give money to organizations that go and fulfill a mission, or are we reaching out to people ourselves? It doesn't have to be either/or— it can and even should be both/and, because some organizations can reach where individuals can't—but there's deep danger of creating a chasm where we feel we're fulfilling enough of a mission, even the

Great *Com*mission, when we simply give money to a church or Christian entity and then walk away.

But what mission field can *we* serve on with our own hands and feet?

Can we take the Good News to the hurting in our cities?

Can we sow into a local homeless or halfway shelter with our time, talents, or money?

Are there hurting people we can serve personally, not just by investing into a church they might one day attend?

Not every missionary is called to serve in Guatemala or Haiti or Honduras. We are ambassadors for Christ, missionaries to our modern world. No overseas travel needed! And we are tasked with taking the Gospel to those on our mission field with the boldness, vigor, and determination of any cross-borders traveler.

We may not have to go as far, but we still have *far* to go.

Where can you sow? Where can you fulfill the mission?

Locally? Nationally? In your own backyard?

To what mission field is God calling YOU?

This Week's Prayer: Yahweh, thank You for calling us all to mission fields both near and far. Help me to find the mission fields where I can serve best with my unique talents...and help me serve well on them! Amen.

FAITH LIVED OUT

HAVE YOU EVER MET SOMEONE, then gotten to know them better only to find yourself surprised to learn that they were a *Christian?* And I don't mean in a good way!

There's a great percentage of those, especially in the younger generation, who identify as Christians only because their parents went to church. But just as there are many who are Christian by inheritance, not by choice, there are many who claim and believe they are Christ-followers to their core—yet their behavior says otherwise.

If Christ is our vine and we are his branches, we will produce fruit in accordance with that. If we want to display the love and power of God accurately, we have to not just have faith, but live it out. This will produce in us love, joy, peace, patience, kindness, goodness, faithfulness, gentleness, and self-control. All these traits should shine out of us at any given moment, making not *us*, but *Christ in us*, attractive to people.

When I meet people, I don't always lead with, "Hi, I'm Renee, and by the way I'm a Christian!" That's bound to come up eventually—I'm not shy about my faith!—but my prayer is always that when the subject arises organically, my behavior will in no way have been contradictory to my profession.

When we live out our faith, not just preach it, it offers another avenue for Jesus to reach people and for people to find Truth. The discipline, boldness, and self-sacrifice involved in walking out the faith we hold is not a simple task...indeed, it requires so much of us we may sometimes feel overwhelmed by it! But if we don't learn to live this way, then our faith becomes a sound bite, a blip in a life otherwise lived for self. We become just another one of "those Christians"—a reason for those who do not yet follow Christ to turn their attention further away from him.

If anyone is surprised I'm a Christian, I want it to be because they've never met Jesus before the way I'm preaching him.

And then, God willing, I'll be able to live by example enough that I can lead them into his open arms.

This Week's Prayer: Yahweh, thank You for the powerful opportunity to witness for You and Your Son with how I live my life! Help me to live it well, bringing more and more people into Your family.

Amen.

LET THEM WANDER

THERE'S SOMETHING SO COMFORTING ABOUT tradition within the Church—one generation following the next, and the next, and the next; tried-and-true creeds, hymns and platitudes passed down through an enduring congregation.

Tradition has churned out a good deal of faithful, God-fearing men and women. It's not difficult to see the value in it.

But there has been a sharp shift in how church is done with the more recent generations. Many are walking out their faith outside the normal parameters of church.

People with love for Jesus and a heart for music aren't just becoming Christian artists, they're becoming secular singers with a message of truth woven into their lyrics. They're artists rendering, not the Christian Bookstore Jesus of soft eyes and creamy skin, but portraits of anguish and sin with a light from Heaven shining through.

As a mid-twentysomething, I was deep in the trenches of the discomfort and even distrust aimed at my generation from its elders. It's not that they didn't believe the spirit of God was in us—they just questioned if our faith should be walked out *that way*. After all, being *in* the world has historically almost become synonymous with being *of* it. So, if you're going to be a Christian *and a writer*, you need to be a Christian writer. As in, books published in the Christian fiction section, please!

At best, my generation and the ones after us have been said to need greater guidance and coaching. We've needed to be reined in. At worst, I've heard it said we're wandering. By investing our talents somewhere other than the mainstream Christian circuit, we are wandering away from the fold.

But sometimes what's called "wandering" is not wandering away from *faith* so much as it's wandering away from *tradition*.

I'd rather be led by God in the wandering wilderness than sit in a pew and never hear His voice. And I hear Him clearest when I'm writing books no Christian fiction section would contain.

Why? Well, because I'm often called to write to those outside the Church who aren't going to hear messages of *agape* love or real redemption or repentance or change anywhere else. They certainly won't ever look at the Christian fiction section!

And the more I talk to others in my generation, the more I hear a common call rising up among us like a prayer chant in the wilderness.

Our talents are meant for so much more than just the beauty of sowing back into our home or local church. They're for growing the Body.

This is true of every generation. Few people understood when my mom hitched a ride to a place she'd never been, with people she'd never met, to begin her journey to move the Word over the world.

Yet her talents in music and art and service were called to something larger than her Catholic upbringing, the church she'd been raised in. She felt the call. She heeded it. And because she did, I now get to raise *my* son in the truth she ardently pursued...even when her family thought she was just wandering away.

So if a beloved young Christian in your life is considering sowing their God-given talents somewhere other than the traditional church setting...let them. Watch them, pray for them, council with them, be with them. But let their talents be water on the parched soil of a dying generation. God has made them missionaries, not overseas, but into the hearts and minds of their peers.

It may be a different mission field than what you've seen before. But it's the one we've got to walk out. And we ask you to pray for us as we work out the mission God has called us to.

This Week's Prayer: Yahweh, thank You for leading even those who seem to wander! Help me, even in my own wanderings, to always be on a mission from You, bringing Your light to any place I roam! Amen.

WHAT'S IN A NAME?

I CAN'T HELP IT; THE second my husband says my full name, even in a casual way, I tense up. Hearing him call me something other than the other pet names I'm used to makes me feel like a kid in trouble.

Growing up, I lived on nicknames, everything from Sunshine Lady to Sparkplug (it's a long story), and the only time anyone ever used my actual name—or *first and middle name, gulp!*—was when I was in trouble...or when they didn't like me enough to use a nickname.

These days, when meeting new people for the first time, I usually introduce myself as "Renee—but you can call me Nay."

So when I read Shakespeare's age-old question "What's in a name?", my first thought is, "A lot, Billy-boy."

I think God would agree. Names crop up in His Word in a variety of ways—the names people were born with, the names they gave to places, the *new* names that spelled new chapters in their lives.

Think Saul/Paul, Abram/Abraham, Simon/Peter.

Think Daniel, Hananiah, Mishael, and Azariah; though they were young Judaic rulers, the latter three are to this day better known by the names given to them in captivity—Shadrach, Meshach, and Abednego.

We're also told Jesus has been given a name known only to him and the Father, and in the future we will each receive a secret name of equal importance.

With all this emphasis around names in the Scriptures and in our lives, we cannot overlook one name mentioned more than any other—over *six thousand* times. And yet there is a great portion of Christianity that doesn't know or refuses to use this name, for one reason or another.

The name is Yahweh.

It is the name of our Father God.

I heard a teaching once about the sheer relational importance of names—Yahweh's included. It's something I connect to personally because of the visceral reaction in me when people use my full name.

How much more for our Yahweh God when so many of His children's tongues are trained not to speak His name, a name He shares with us in His Word over six thousand times!

I certainly felt convicted when I heard that teaching about the importance of *Yahweh's* name. Because we, of course, always want to show Him the respect He's owed...and sometimes respect is to call someone by the name they go by!

What joy it must bring Yahweh when we call the name He gave us, a loving Father sharing such an intimate part of His being. We are told in Scripture that our hairs are numbered and our names known by Jesus and the Father, every individual among us—and we know His.

Now all of us together, let's call on the name of Yahweh, our Father!

This Week's Prayer: Yahweh, thank You for the beauty of Your name and the intimacy of knowing it! Help me to be mindful of how I speak to You, and by what name and title...each and every beautiful one! Amen.

HOW TO REACH PEOPLE WITH THE GOSPEL

EVERY DAY WE ARE SURROUNDED by discomfort, faced with the ways the world rejects the precepts of Yahweh and chooses to go down its own path.

We have the commission to make disciples within a world where barriers are already erected against people of faith. Some of these predispositions are fabricated and undeserved; others are understandable based on the historic content of a Christian faith that hasn't always been Christ-like.

Regardless of the suppositions about Jesus-followers, our task is the same: to make disciples. Discipling means taking the first step, which is inviting people into a relationship with Jesus. But that takes preparation and intentionality on our part.

While our lives should be a witness for Jesus, we can't expect to skate by on fulfilling Jesus's commission by hoping someone, someday, takes notice and comes to him because of that.

We have to act. And we need to act in a way that brings glory and honor to God.

Here are four encouragements to bear in mind as you reach out into a chaotic world and invite people into relationship with Christ. Four things that will help you be a better witness for Christ.

1. **Recognize you're no better than the people you're trying to reach.**

I think we all know this logically, but in practice it's easy to slip into behaving more like the Pharisee than the tax collector in Jesus's tale of Luke 18, patting ourselves on the backs for the misdeeds we don't perform rather than repenting for the ones we're guilty of.

Wallowing in self-degradation doesn't do anyone any good—it certainly doesn't help us be effective witnesses or active disciples of Jesus—but it's important to keep a realistic perspective of ourselves.

At no time in this current life will we be free from flaws, and in coming to Jesus we aren't stripped of the temptation to sin. That comes later.

For now, we are no better than anyone we seek to reach with the Good News of Jesus. It's *Jesus* who is better, and we are in a unique place through the righteousness imparted by our union with him to show others that while we remain flawed, while we are still dust and ashes, Jesus is raising us up to be seated with him in glory.

It's not to us that we want to draw people, because within our flesh we have nothing great to offer. Remember that you're drawing people to Jesus, and always be honest with them and yourself that you shine not your own goodness, but the light of him.

2. **Practice the lost art of love in listening.**

Being heard is something too many people don't get enough of. I remember the first time a mentor pressed through a flippant comment I made and asked, "Why did you say that?"

Stunned, I hardly knew how to respond. By that time, I was used to my brush-off remarks, which often hid a deeper well of feeling than I could openly express, being ignored. But this person tunneled deep, listening to every word I said and digging out not just parts of me I'd been afraid to face until then, but a sense of purpose I'd never felt before.

When we listen without the need to either pontificate or defend, we open the door to honest, loving dialogue. We create a sense of safety through which real, deep self-awareness and healing come about. In our willingness to be listeners, we can help create an environment of visceral quiet, inside which people hear the still, small voice of God.

Learn to listen in a way that's about the other person, not about the point you want to make.

3. **Don't conflate the magnitude of struggles you aren't tempted by.**

A friend once asked me why many Christians condemn homosexuality so fiercely and publicly, why that seems to be the hill they're willing to die on, but adulterers are much more easily forgiven—

despite Levitical law demanding the same punishment for both.

After taking it to the Lord in prayer and pondering her question, the conclusion I came to is this: it's a lot easier to shine a harsh spotlight on the temptations we don't personally struggle with. The things that are a non-issue for us as individuals, we tend to aggrandize, slipping all too effortlessly into the mindset of "Maybe I do this, but at least I don't do *that*." And that's an odious attitude to those who follow Jesus and those who don't.

A person who struggles with sexual temptation is no less worthy of God's redeeming love than one who deals with pride or covetousness or lying. Resist the temptation to shed harsher light on the things you aren't specifically tempted with. Remember that all temptations, all sin, all shortcomings are covered under the blood of Christ's sacrifice and subject to the redemptive power of his healing love.

It's not our job to judge one sin as worse than another. It's our job to bring Jesus's light and love to all so they're set free from *whatever* sin and temptation they may struggle with.

4. **Lead with love.**

Remember the saying "people don't care how much you know until they know how much you care"? Knowledge is a blessing and a curse, because it's really easy to lead with what you know, assuming it will stitch up someone's wounds before you ever have to get close enough for them to bleed on you.

Yet we live in a time where the first step to healing for many is not a chapter-and-verse recitation, but a shoulder to cry on.

A friend told me once that "People change when they're uncomfortable." I've heard others use this as sort of a witnessing method; they'll toss out Scripture references about topics to make people uncomfortable in hopes they'll change.

Yet in my own experience, the discomfort that invokes change is not the kind that comes from feeling like someone's holding a knife to my neck. It's the gentle, insistent, evocative pressure of Christ's love, the kindness of God that brings about lasting change. (Rom. 2:4)

If we try to make people uncomfortable by telling them they're going to hell, they may change, but it's likely to be a tiring, taxing, maybe even impermanent shift.

On the other hand, introducing people to the love of God opens the door for Him to work the soil of their hearts for an enduring, deep, personal change. Our job is to lead with that love.

Before you talk to a woman about her choice to terminate her pregnancy, sit with her and get to know the why. Before you lob verses about modesty and promiscuity at a person dressed a certain way, learn what the personal payoff is in what the surface portrays. Before you tell someone about what God wants from them, listen to their story. Take time to see the person, not just the conduct, not just the sin.

Remember that once upon a time, someone had to see beneath your inherent flaws, your walls and barriers, your past. Whether Jesus cracked through it himself or someone did it in his name, it started with you. You were worth getting to know, your heart was worth pursuing. And so is theirs.

We will never be perfect in our witness for Christ. We will stumble, we may stammer, we will definitely say the wrong thing from time to time.

But with ears open to listen, a heart open to love, feet grounded in the truth of who and what we are, and a clear understanding of how far we've come and how far we have to go, we are in a good position to invite others into the journey with us.

And we are certainly better equipped to help them see Jesus as we go along the Road to Emmaus together, the Redeemer walking beside us both to open the eyes of saved and unsaved alike to the truth of his wondrous love.

This Week's Prayer: Yahweh, thank You for empowering and equipping Your people to bring the Gospel to the world! Help me to do this in a way that's full of love for everyone I meet and brings a fantastic report of You! Amen.

THE DOG WHO ATE MY GUM

I KNEW SOMETHING WAS WRONG the moment I walked inside the house.

The distinct lack of our ten-year-old dog, Bay, coming to greet me was clue number one.

Clue number two came in the form of a packet of gum with several pieces ripped out, lying in the middle of the living room floor. Some bits were half-chewed, some not. I guess his conquest didn't agree with him.

Sighing heavily, I called Bay once. Twice. Three times.

Some people say animals aren't all that clever, but Bay knew he'd done wrong. The moment he came out into the hall and saw the empty gum wrapper in my hand, he froze. Then he averted his gaze and licked his lips. Finally, he sloooowly sat down, tail sheepishly thumping the floor.

How did he know he'd misbehaved? Simple. This was (*by far*) not the first time my husband and I had chastised old Bay on his food-raiding habits. Whatever family had him for the eight years before he became our boy, they taught him stealing food was a no-no, too.

But he kept doing it anyway. He just couldn't seem to help himself.

Scolding a dog for misbehaving is one of my least-favorite things to do, right down there with eating lima beans and setting up doctor's appointments. Yet even when I no-no'd Bay, reminding him gum is really not good for dogs (as if he could actually understand me, I know), I felt not anger, but an overwhelming amount of love.

Isn't that just like God and us?

If my Bay was a food-raider, I'm a sin-raider. I know I shouldn't do X, Y, or Z. I know these things are bad for me, that they get me in trouble, that they're against what God wants me to do and what He wants *for* me. Yet, like the Apostle Paul, I find myself drawn back frequently into that pattern of doing the things I don't want to do. Stealing food off the sin-table. Ripping into all the garbage of life.

I'm like Bay. I just can't seem to help myself.

I used to wonder a lot more often how God could still love me when I'm such a hopeless repeat-offender, such a chronic sin-raider. But slowly I gained greater and greater understanding as I interacted with an old dog who just couldn't—and never did—learn the new trick of leaving food or the garbage can untouched.

I scolded him knowing he was likely going to get in trouble again. I cleaned up every mess with full awareness it wouldn't be the last one ever. And as I watched Bay avoid my gaze, tail and ears drooping sadly, I remembered that he and I weren't so different. Whatever that thing is in us that compels us to do what we shouldn't, in the end what we both needed was a firm word and gentle love.

How does God still love me despite my sin?

Simple. For the same reason I loved Bay even when he misbehaved.

Because I'm His, as Bay was mine.

This Week's Prayer: Yahweh, thank You for loving me even at my lowest, when sin is a constant struggle in my life. Help me to do better, so that I can avoid the same track of sin over and over, and can continue to grow in service to You! Amen.

HOW DO YOU IDENTIFY?

IT'S LIKELY HAPPENED TO EACH of us at some point in our lives. Upon finding ourselves in a situation that made us uncomfortable in one way or another, we were relieved to see someone else who made us feel safe.

Maybe we knew them—maybe we didn't. But something about them made us think, "Ah! There's one of *my* people." It could be someone:

- Dressed as casually as you at an event.
- Wearing a pop culture t-shirt like yours.
- Being the same ethnicity.
- Professing the same political leanings.
- Carrying themselves in a similar manner.
- Filling the same profession.
- Being your same gender.

Whatever the likeness is, in that moment, you feel just a little less uncomfortable, because there's someone present with whom you identify.

Identity is one of the single most important matters for many people today, and also one that must be navigated with some of the greatest care— because **the things by which you identify yourself have power over you.**

This is true across any spectrum. If you identify with any group, any tribe, any faction, you enter in under their auspices. Their causes are at least *expected,* if not required, to be yours. What they stand for, you are expected to stand for.

After all, how can you identify as conservative if you don't support conservative values? How can you call yourself progressive if you don't stand for what the progressive platform stands for?

To identify as a writer, you must write. As a musician, you must play music. You can't call yourself a Marvel fan if you don't even *like Marvel movies*, dude.

And there's the catch: to identify as something, we must give it power over us. Power to define us. Power to, at least in some way, control our actions, thoughts, and choices. We become prone to shifting our patterns to fit the mold.

So if someone says "real writers write *every day regardless of how they feel*"—well, I want to be a *real writer*, don't I? If that means sitting at my keyboard hating myself on my bad days just so I can say I wrote *something* and therefore I can identify as a *real writer*...that's just part of the job, isn't it? The pain is now part of my identity.

If you want to identify as a cool kid, you'd better do what the cool kids do. Today it's the clothing you wear. Tomorrow it's the alcohol you drink and the drugs you take.

If you want to be a tough guy on the street, today it's intimidating a stranger. Tomorrow it's robbing them.

Next thing you know, the things you identify as are dictating your way of life. You lose all sense of self, of the identity you were striving for, because the movement doesn't care about the individual. It exists to perpetuate itself.

God is pretty concerned with where we draw our identity from. In Galatians 3, He tells us this: "There is neither Jew nor Greek, there is neither slave nor free, there is neither male nor female, for you all are one in Christ Jesus."

This was as revolutionary the day Paul penned it as it is to us now. Where you drew your identity from in the ancient world defined quite a bit of who you were and how far you could go. Until Jesus came and fulfilled the law, the Jews alone had claim to the promises of God and hope for that future. The distinction between opportunities for males and females back then was even more profound than it is today. And need I say anything about the different opportunities for the slave and free man?

Yet God was saying this: when we draw our identity from Jesus, the division of sects and segments—the things by which many define themselves—are torn away. The people under Christ are not merely *our people*, we are all *one people*. No one is better than another within God's family. It is true, absolute, utter equality and wholeness.

In the broader spiritual reality laid out by God, there are two identities: those who are in Christ and those who are not—yet. Our concern should be to disciple as many as we can under *that* identity...under the banner of Jesus.

In the end, it is the only identity that matters. Everything else is finite, impermanent, and imperfect, liable to lead us astray into causes we don't want to support, into actions not aligned to God's will, into mindsets and motives that are not healthy.

By contrast, when you draw your identity from who you are in Christ, your foundation is solid. When planted in this, the need to draw a sense of self from the ever-changing currents of culture and tribe and segment within the world fades away. That is our true identity, stamped into our spirit at the moment we made Jesus our Lord.

Let's never forget that. It's the truth of who we are.

This Week's Prayer: Yahweh, thank You that even in confused and difficult times, my identity is found in You! Please help me not to get caught up in the search for who I am or can be—help me to instead grow from the knowledge that I am Yours and Christ's! Amen.

CHRIST, OUR PEACE

DURING THE HOLIDAYS, THE WORD everyone both secular and religious seems to leap on is "peace"—specifically peace on earth, and good will as spoken by the angel at the birth of Christ (Luke 2:14).

Why is peace such an important subject? For many, it's because they recognize the lack of peace throughout the world. Chaos finds us irrespective of age, race, gender, creed, career, etc.

Everyone could use a little more peace in their lives. But there are numerous times that the perfect truth of Scripture makes it clear: simple human "peace" is not enough. We need a heavenly peace that passes understanding in order to experience true soul-rest in contentment and security.

Before Jesus ascended to the Father's right hand, one of the last things he gave to his followers was *peace*. In fact, he emphasized that he was leaving *his* peace with them, and not as the world gives it (John 14:27). In Philippians 4:7, Paul exhorts the reader that, specifically through our union with Christ, we will have peace that passes understanding.

When the Book of Isaiah listed the attributes of the then-future Messiah, one of them was that he would be the *prince of peace* (Isaiah 9:6). And the braiding together of perfect peace and the presence of Christ has quite literally been a highlight of his very existence since the angel first announced his birth to the shepherds in Luke 2.

This aspect of Jesus's purpose and character is driven home again in Ephesians, where Paul speaks of the union of Jews and Gentiles in Christ. Emphasis is placed on the fact that Jesus Christ is our peace—the sense of unity in the spirit and peace among

Christians comes through Jesus and not by our *own* sense of these things.

And why not?

Because it can't. Because our concept of peace is limited by our fallen state. Because we often think of peace as something we can hold only with those who see eye-to-eye with us, or who live up to our standards, or by some other arbitrary delineation. We are incapable of experiencing true peace personally or *inter*personally if it does not come through the scope of Christ—his teachings, his dealings, and how he works with us all.

Jesus brought a new sense of peace to the world. He died on the cross, opening a path to perfect peace in union with him, and through him, with the Father. He also encourages his followers to live peaceably among others as much as they can, even going so far as to love their enemies and pray for those who persecute them!

Notice that having peace in Christ does not mean we will be free of trouble—it's broader and more beautiful than that. It's that *even* in times of distress, doubt, persecution, and struggle, we can still be peaceful with our trust firmly placed in Christ and God.

So when you're feeling troubled, particularly if you are living in a state of contention with a fellow believer, ask yourself whose peace you're truly relying on: your own, or Christ's? Are you upholding him as your peace, or striving for a personal sense of solace and unity that comes through the human perspective—the peace the world tries to offer?

Jesus gave us many examples in his teachings here on earth of how to live peaceably with one another despite our differences, as well as with those currently outside the Body of Christ. He also speaks with us through the holy spirit dwelling in us. He can and *will* show you the path to peace through him, who is himself *our peace.*

And what peace there is in knowing we do not have to strive for these things alone.

This Week's Prayer: Yahweh, thank You for sending Your Son to be our peace! Thank You that I do not have to strive for peace alone. Help me embrace and live in that peace! Amen.

COME BOLDLY BEFORE GOD

WITH CHRISTMAS JUST AROUND THE corner, the mood among many Christians is polarized. Some are those abounding in joy and excitement, what most people call "the Christmas spirit"; and there are others who are "not really feeling it," who are stressed, overwhelmed, feeling rushed or underappreciated...or perhaps even grieving. Some are facing their first Christmas without a loved one, their first Christmas alone, or a Christmas with the shadow of a diagnosis, discord, relational rift, or an uncertain future ahead.

This time of year, many Christians set aside time and focus to celebrate the birth of Christ. Sometimes I'm not sure we grasp the broader picture of that: what was set into motion on that glorious day. How the purpose of the ages began to be fulfilled with the coming of Jesus, and how just a few decades later, the greatest secret gift of all time would be unwrapped: the part that the Gentiles would have in God's family.

Ephesians 3:11-12 tells us that "[The wisdom of God revealed through the construction of His church] was consistent with his purpose throughout the ages that he accomplished in Christ Jesus our Lord, in whom we have boldness and access to God with confidence through our trust in him."

With the purpose of the ages accomplished in Christ, we have access to God which was hitherto unknown. Our God is not far off to us, He is near. We can have boldness in that; we can confidently approach God because our trust in Jesus forged a bridge between broken man and the perfect Creator.

So as Christmas draws near, I want to encourage, specifically, those who are downtrodden, unhappy, and afraid, to boldly approach God and give it all to

Him. All of your burdens, all of your cares...through your trust in Jesus, lay them at the Father's feet. They are too heavy for you to carry alone. But as we all reflect on what significance the birth of Christ had and still has on the world, let's also embrace what significance his sacrifice and resurrection brought: the closing of the gap between us and God, which allows us to access Him with everything that weighs us down. To surrender it to Him.

You are a part of His purpose for the ages. You are a part of His family. And at this time of year, when peace and good will are so close at heart, I encourage us all to seek the peace that can be found nowhere else but through trust in Jesus and in the loving arms of the Father.

Merry Christmas!

This Week's Prayer: Yahweh, thank You for sending Your Son and for the culmination of Your purposes that came with his birth! Help me to never forget that I can now boldly come before you thanks to his sacrifice! Amen.

YOUR PURPOSE IN THE PURPOSE

SPENDING A YEAR LOOKING DEEP into the Book of Ephesians at the encouragement of a mentor taught me a lot about the depths and richness of the story God built into this world and this life; about our standing with Him, with Jesus, with each other; about the grace we've been given and how we should walk out our lives in response to that grace.

One thing I've learned and will never forget is that we each have a purpose to fulfill within the purpose of God—the plan of the ages.

Do you think you're insignificant? A tack-on to the aftermath of the plan? An inconsequential droplet of ink cast off on the corner of the page, of no value to the story of the ages woven together since the beginning of time?

Because you are not. You are a member in particular of the Body of Christ, part of the holy habitat built of the family of God. You are:

- One of the dead awakened to new life
- Part of God's team
- Adopted
- Paid for by the blood
- Defined by your identity in Jesus Christ who you serve
- Walking alive
- Covered in the peace of Jesus
- Prayed for by believers who came before you, and by Christ himself (John 17)
- Rooted and grounded in love, so you can come boldly before God
- Not a stranger, forgotten, or inconsequential
- Ransomed from darkness to light

And now it's time to fix on your armor and *stand*. Seek God. Imitate Jesus. Embrace your purpose within the purpose of the ages and walk it out in a way worthy of the calling to which you've been called. We are here, we are home in Christ, we are one Body with no walls between us, planned before the foundations of the world, called and redeemed, fearfully and wonderfully made.

It's time to cast off the shackles of death and walk alive, brothers and sisters. It's time to do what we were made to do: to bring the truth of Jesus, the love of God, and the story of redemption to hungry hearts all over the world.

This Week's Prayer: Yahweh, thank You for all the work You did to bring about redemption in the world. Thank You for calling us forth into a better way of living! Please help me to conduct my life in a way that glorifies and honors You and Your Son and continues the good work of Christ! Amen.

About
R.S. Dugan

R. S. Dugan joined the Spirit & Truth team as a volunteer in 2008 and has since become a staff member assisting with administration, heading up the Writer's Network, and contributing to the content pool with written works of her own, which is her greatest passion both on and off the job.

An Indiana native, wife, and mother, she is excited to share that passion with future generations and with her own, particularly through the written word. In her free time, Renee loves writing novels, spending time with her family and friends, and visiting every small-town coffee shop she can find.

About
Spirit & Truth

SPIRIT & TRUTH is a worldwide, multimedia, multigenerational learning platform helping people become like Christ together through videos, podcasts, articles, blogs, social media networking, a Bible translation and commentary project, a virtual learning center, online and local fellowships, regional and national events, and more. This effort is spearheaded by a team of varying ages from different walks of life and backgrounds, unified around the goal of helping people experience transformative relationships with God, Jesus Christ, themselves, their families, and the Body of Christ.